GRACE HAPPENS

A Guide to Living Fearlessly

By Lane Kennedy

Acknowledgments and Thank You's

This small book has been a group effort. Yes, I may have channeled and wrote it but without the courage, willingness and creative spirits of so many women, this book would not have been created or completed.

Thank you to All of my clients, you know who you are, thank you.

Grace Happens when you trusted me and allowed me the opportunity to guide you to Presence, connecting you to your inner voice. You continue to be brave, and I am so grateful to have witnessed your lives unfold fearlessly.

Thank you Stef Tousignant, for being a friend who said yes, to showing up year after year with me and for saying yes to creating the beautiful book jacket. Your creative genius knew best! Thank you.

Laura Belzer, you have an eye like no other. Thank you for your frankness and making me find time to take a new photo, your photography skills slay!

Thank you Tracy Benjamin, for the simplicity of your lettering and handwriting. I believe it's women like you who foster creativity in others that will keep our world alive.

Alicia Lynch, for reading and rereading and gently nudging me to completion. Thank you for not letting me hit publish without reading and rereading and editing. Your constant poking, facial expressions and non judgmental questions asked me to rise up and become a better teacher. Thank you.

Thank you to my husband, the man I love, who offers me space to find my way, alone and next to me at my side, when needed.

My kiddo. You inspire me to be a better human, I am so thankful to you for being kind to my spirit and always bringing jokes to my stressful times, you know me like no other.

The First 100 who were lucky enough to connect, lean in, write, share and believe that there was / and is something greater working in all our lives. Thank you.

TABLE OF CONTENTS

Introduction *Prologue*

Chapter 1 Are You Ready to Change?

Chapter 2 Finding Your Voice and Emotional Awareness

Chapter 3 Learning to Become Vulnerable and Emotionally Naked

Chapter 4 Getting Honest with Yourself

Chapter 5 Choosing Acceptance in Order to Grow

Chapter 6 Cultivating Inner Strength

Chapter 7 Finding and Implementing Your Worth

Chapter 8 Following Your Own Path in Confidence

Chapter 9 Finding Your True North; The Culmination

Chapter 10 Revealing More & Closure

Resources

*Hello Friend, thank you for finding me. I've written this book as a conversation, I hope you read it as such, and if you want to have a live conversation with me, please reach out to me on my website. Once you have read the chapters and completed catching up with yourself, I invite you to share with me here: https://lanekennedy.com/contact-lane what shifted, or not? Perhaps you will put this book down, and someone else will pick it up, whatever the journey of this little guide book is I hope it brings guidance and joy in living a fearless life. Grace Happens, allow her.

With Much Love & Appreciation.

Lane

INTRODUCTION

Why Grace? *Grace Happens*. Grace is a state of being, a sense of calm before and after the storm, a place you want to be when you're tired and or awake. Grace is peace in your heart, prayers answered and a deep sense of knowing that *yes*, you are good, that your life is on track, exactly how it's meant to be. In fact you are exactly in the right time at the right moment, yes, *Grace Happens* in time on time, and perhaps that is not on your timeline but you go with it. You lean in, listen and trust. Grace lives is in the ethers of your being, she is mysterious; some say spiritual. Your job is tapping in and letting her guide you to all the possibilities of your amazing life.

You're done playing small, aren't you? You have absolute permission to be more, have more, and live more fully. All you have to do is reach and work for it; simple but not easy. But—I believe you can do anything if you set your mind to it. Are you ready for that? Let's begin. Get ready to think bigger and play more! First, I have to say: thank you for allowing me into your life and picking up this small book! Over the next few chapters, you will get to know a little more about me, my journey, and why I wrote this book for you. It's been a long time in the making! I'd put my money on a bet that you're reading this book because you want change, am I right? You want something different. You've already attempted twenty different courses, eight different therapies, and read through hundreds of self-help books. You've tried and failed. You feel like nothing will ever change, nothing works, and something is still wrong. With this guide/book as a roadmap (not a predetermined one), you will:

- Set your own course
- Uncover your inner wisdom
- Tell the truth
- Open your heart
- Step into alignment
- Discover your strengths
- Take the necessary actions to lean into more of your authentic self
- Allow Grace to Happen
- Live with Presence

There will be no more loneliness, no more overwhelm, no more hesitation when it comes to making decisions, no more ache of uncertainty, and no more hangovers from one too many glasses of wine to simply take the edge off your long day. In this book, I will be sharing stories about some of my clients. I have asked them for permission to share their journeys with you, and they have graciously agreed. All names have been changed in order to protect their privacy. Let me back up a little and share with you about this book—how I began my journey and why I put it together. I've personally helped thousands of people live more fearlessly, find balance, build self-confidence, and upgrade their habits while guiding them to what they want (or rather how they want to BE and live a fulfilled life). It's been an incredible journey and one in which I'm privileged and honored to take part.

Breakthroughs happen when your Soul is ready. They don't necessarily happen when you plan for them, or even when you spend hours thinking about some epic change. Hang tight, you're ready for this. Let's get started.

Allow Grace to happen!

"I'm simply here to serve, but will someone tell me what to do." Anonymous

PROLOGUE: MY STORY

Before I started modeling or entered the startup world, and consulting, I was small and shy. The epitome of a wallflower. I wanted to be noticed; I just didn't have what the other girls had. I wasn't raised with a set of rules on how to behave or a book of how-to's. Self-confidence wasn't really instilled in me.

I had no supervision because my mom left us when I was five years old. Unfortunately, or fortunately, depending on how you want to look at it, no one in my life stepped in to take her place. No one told me what was happening the first time I had my menstrual cycle or how to deal with the mess and stain in my clothing. I had no idea what was happening to my body the first time I kissed a boy.

As a result of some unfortunate events that occurred in my family life, I was tossed into adulthood somewhat early. At thirteen, I became awkwardly acquainted with emotions that were never discussed in our family, and for the first time, I was afraid. I lived in fear every day. I was completely reluctant to speak in groups, fearful of saying the wrong words or dressing out of style.

I was sure that I would select the wrong colors and look like I was dressed by a crazy person! The voices in my head surely didn't help me. They constantly nagged me about my hair, my face, the pimples that never went away, and my chubby body. I wasn't skinny enough. I wasn't blonde enough either. Let's not forget I was only thirteen. What was a girl to do?

I had to change. I had to find something much greater to help me be in this world, to help me feel like I could do something with myself. I prayed. I know that sounds crazy, but it's true. I jumped on the Jesus bandwagon. I snuck out at night to sing in the youth rock choir and played hooky on the weekends to attend the youth revival sessions. Now don't go anywhere; don't leave me— please keep reading! I am only telling you this so you get a glimpse of how desperate I was to feel better. I wanted to feel like I was a part of something (I'm not knockin' religion, don't get me wrong). I wanted to fit in; I wanted to know the answers. My youth evangelism didn't last long, but what stuck with me from those early "Can I get an Amen" days is the important part. I learned that I am just like everyone else. Looking for something or someone to connect with, and that I am an imperfect person seeking perfection. Whoa—total game-changer— Seeking!

Over the years I've been fortunate enough to travel to a myriad of countries and taste unusual exotic foods— like beetles, brains, and grasshoppers. I've watched people survive horrendous conditions, such as a girl being sold into prostitution so that her older sister could have plastic surgery. The surgery enabled her to be married off to a wealthy family. Another woman I spoke with had to live through her daughter being abducted and murdered. I've been humbled and honored to listen to these heart-wrenching, life-changing stories.

Some say that I'm quiet while others will tell you I'm the life of the party and the glue that keeps everything together. My perspective on me? Well that's useless, isn't it —or is it? I can only share my experience, and that's what I want you to *feel* in this notebook. I can share with you that from a young age I was interpreted as being a little different. I was different from my classmates and my best friends. Most of my friends were interested in shoving off to Ivy League schools and getting degrees. I wasn't interested in attending a privileged university and getting a fancy degree that I would most likely never use in any part of my life.

I was too excited to be out on my own! I wanted to be out in the world living and experiencing it. I didn't aspire to be holed up in a small dingy dorm room, writing papers and asking classmates for the notes on lectures that I would have never attended. I wasn't interested in the routine of education dedicated to subjects which I just couldn't stomach at the time. After years of judging myself for not being like them, I've finally settled into being confident with the path that I took. I'm in the world now as a result of being a little bit different. I wanted to experience life, taste it, listen to it, and see it from all angles up close and personal.

During the Fall of my seventeenth year, I stood on the BART platform at 8:05 a.m. on a Monday morning, ready to *arrive*. I watched the train doors open. I held my breath and watched them close. That train was headed to San

Francisco, where I had received a full scholarship to fashion school. I was expected to go into a field I wasn't completely sold on, and participate in it for the rest of my life. I loved fashion; I often designed my own outfits. I felt giddy when strangers complimented my clothes. Even still, I was happy I didn't board the BART train that morning. My life could have fallen part right there, I had nothing to fall back on, school was the next step, wasn't it? When I found a tiny ad for an in-house fashion model, I was intrigued. I applied for it.

My first modeling audition brought me a five-year contract with a high profile design team. They taught me everything I needed to know about the fashion world and more. The first time I changed my clothes for money, I had a conscious moment of my decision to live less conventionally. While my friends, neighbors, and roommates were making $800 a month, I was making $8000 a month—in less than a third of the time. I believed that I had indeed *arrived*. I felt happy, and jobs kept coming my way!

I'm not going to bore you with a lot of the details, just make a note to yourself that I've been around and I've never been bored. If I was, it was because I was hungover and couldn't think clearly. I'm not going to drum on about the rock 'n' roll, drug and alcohol infested, bulimic life that I barely survived. But for more than fifteen years, I drank vodka on the rocks with a twist of lemon, I hoarded cases of red wine and snuck in mind-altering pills and white powder. I was trying to escape the truth of my family chaos, my feeling unworthy, my fear of others' opinions of me, or the lurking eyes of strangers. I drank and used drugs to quiet the noise of doubt. To numb the feeling of not being good enough to be in the room with others.

I've had many gut-wrenching hangovers and ugly demoralizing moments, such as the time I came out of a blackout while having sex with my boss. We were on the side of the road, on top of his car in plain daylight, and mind you—he was married with two young children. I've lived through icy chills, sweating buckets of tears while wrapped around someone else's toilet, not knowing if I was going to make it as I heaved more yellow bile. I've had countless moments waking up next to strangers, both men and women, married and not married; numerous occasions of not knowing where my car was, afraid to find it, fearing wreckage; limitless times of total confusion, questioning where my clothes had gone, where my money had gone, and how did I get home?

My life, as I see it, is mysterious with a lot of peaks and valleys. I've danced cheek to cheek with the design icon Tom Ford, drunk delicious cocktails with Madonna, mocktails with Herb Ritts, shared Thanksgiving turkey dinner with Ellen Degeneres, and lived with Sharon Stone. Some people would say I've had quite an exceptional life, but I suppose it's a matter of perspective. I am not sharing this information in hopes you will think differently of me—or like me anymore or any less. I only share it with the promise of you understanding that anything is possible in your life! I look at life with possibility and know in my heart that I am capable of doing anything, just like you. You are capable! You have a heart—and that is what will attract your desires.

One chilly night, I remember drinking and driving home at 1:55 in the morning, the bars just closed. With the windows down and my head out the window, I prayed as I drove East on Fountain towards Pink's hot dogs in Los Angeles. I was desperate. Dying, I thought. I was seeking a miracle that would relieve me of the alcohol poisoning that I had numbingly done to myself. Perhaps grilled onions and a greasy hotdog would cure me. As I reflect, I can clearly see that the miracle would be me making it to my destination and parking the car without hitting anyone.

Definition: Grace Happens. A moment of mysterious action or thought that changes the course of one's life.

By pure Grace, I was never pulled over for driving under the influence. Moreover, I've never killed anybody while driving drunk, and pray that drunk driving stops for everyone. This all seems to be a part of the mystery of (my) life; it doesn't make sense to me. If I drew a line from point A to B, the line definitely wouldn't be straight. The facts are undeniably true: I shouldn't be here. I had an inability to say *no* to anything that could alter my thoughts and feelings. There was no way that I would have listened to you if you told me that by changing one habit—drinking alcohol—my life would change. It would become something beyond my wildest dreams, and completely unrecognizable.

I guess that's more of what this book is about—the series of experiences leading me and others to accept that there is something more in life worth living for. I call it, "Being Connected." I also call it *Grace*. Your ability to listen deeply to the Universe. How many times in your life has it all come together? The rent was paid on time even when your bank account was at zero, the boss gave you a pass for being late one more time, the car started after you drove for miles on empty, you didn't get in an accident on your way home last night after having a few too many... Life is a continual mystery. Are you paying attention or letting these moments of *Grace* pass you by?

Over the years, I've discovered that for me there's a theme of dissatisfaction with the ordinary; I've been seeking "more" my entire life. Have you? Are you now? A lot of what I help others with is quieting the negativity loops that fire off in the brain. They are always unannounced. This superhighway negativity materializes in an instant. Usually, it's right after something good happens, or right before something important is supposed to happen. I want you to tune in, turn on; pay attention. I will also guide you how to be still through times of desperation, confusion, chaos, and overwhelm. I'm going to attempt to give you everything I've learned through all my clean and sober years of living—without numbing out or hurting my body. Ultimately, it's been about feeling my emotions, identifying them, and then making a decision to change one behavior, at a time. By doing this, I've escaped the mental angst which previously stole years of my life from me.

"Thinking too long about doing something is often the reason it never gets done." Anonymous

CHAPTER 1

Everyone Has a Beginning

Are You Ready to Change?

I'll ask again, *are you ready to change*—and no I'm not going to ask you to stop drinking, that's just what happened to me—are you ready to lose some weight, get healthy, own your own house, leave a broken marriage, start your own business, quit your job, feel amazing in your body... are you? Are you ready to change your life? Let's do this! Let's embark on a journey to co-create an experience that will change you from the inside out.

If I asked you, "Do you know who you truly are?" would you be able to answer that? Do you need help defining what matters to you the most? Have you been paying attention to those little, often drowned out feelings and moments that determine your life? Some people call them moments of grandeur; some say they are greater realizations or passing fancies. I call them subtle game-changing moments. We need them to survive and thrive, and I want you to start paying attention to them. Can you start doing that?

Right now, whether you believe it or not—a reality exists in which you are great, even if you don't think it's true at this very moment. Call it love, a higher power, your North Star—call it what you will, but name it. If I told you I think you are amazing, would you believe me? Could you? Are you amazing? Say, "YES!"

Repeat after me: "I am amazing."

Great job! You've started!

Learning how to believe in your inner wisdom will push you to stop chasing something that is "out there." Every answer you will ever need is deep within you, usually buried beneath years of debris. You have the answers, trust me. I will help you unearth them.

Are you ready to think bigger and take true ownership of your life? Feel empowered in your body? Navigate both emotional and physical obstacles? Let's begin living your life fearlessly, get out on the edge. Discover more of who you are and what you bring to this world.

Just remember, this is a *lifestyle shift*. This is not a "quick fix, I'm just going to try this for a while" type of thing. No, this is an entire life change that you have been looking for. You're done with living in overwhelm, chaos, and too much to do. You're done not feeling quite right, and getting nowhere! You want more from your life, and it's here for you NOW.

Instructions bring clarity.

Here's how this little book works. As you read these pages, I will ask you to trust the process, investigate, uncover, discover, and, yes, to be honest with yourself. As you read these pages you may also want to head over to a special page on my website, https://lanekennedy.com/grace-happens to grab your *bonuses* and extended awareness exercises and meditations I have created for you as a gift to use while on this journey. **Register and use the CODE "Fearless" for access.** While excavating the landscape of your life, you will find the truth of who you are and what you are capable of doing. Remember what I said at the beginning—I believe you're capable of more and that you can do anything. You can have anything your heart desires! You will have to take small steps on this journey, which I call action steps and practice. No one has ever gotten to the other side of a mountain, road, or the world without taking steps and using some navigation.

You will have to take these actions if you truly want a different life. Different results can *only* occur with different actions which change you. Are you thinking it's going to be too much? If so, put this book down now. Save it for another time in your life—when you're ready, when you are tired of being victimized, and you're willing to take action to live your Soul's Divine Desire and Purpose. Yes, it is going to take an effort to change, but I know you can do it.

Your life is epic.

> **Definition: Epic. Heroic or grand in scale or character.**

Your life is meant to be seen and heard. Your thoughts and perspectives are unique. Perhaps you have answers for people who can't get them from anyone else! So stop hiding; it's time. You are on the road to stepping into thinking bigger and transforming. My goal here is to get you to a happier, healthier you, where you are making clear decisions and taking significant actions every day in your (remarkable) life. Oh, and let's not forget, you will also walk away from self-doubt and fear! Heck, you might even stop drinking for a while, start eating more vegetables, run a marathon, or pack up and move to the other side of the world. No more holding back—you've got this in the bag!

As you uncover and search, I ask that you document the actions you take (take photos, email me, or post to Facebook / www.facebook.com/lanekennedy). This not only lets me know that you're serious about making a change in your life, but it also validates what you're doing. You will have proof of your earned success. One of the greatest tools I have in my life is community. It changes everything. Please join me online — https://lanekennedy.com/contact-lane if you can't find me for a cuppa tea in San Francisco.

Oh, and one last mention before we begin. I want you to consider purchasing a notebook or a moleskin to hold all of your findings. You will want to remember this journey, so let's make sure to have it safe somewhere in a bound book—not on tiny Post-It notes or scraps of paper or even on your iPhone. I also want you to schedule time for yourself; color block your calendar with time for YOU. If you're not quite sure how to do this, you can search the web for a post about it.

It's paramount to be in the moment with yourself so that you can reflect and find answers in an organic way. That's it! Simple, right? Now are you ready? I am.

Let's begin!

Let's begin with getting real about where you are at and what you want in your life. Let's start out by admitting where you are in your life today. Before we get into it, I want you to understand the word "admit." Just so you're not confused in any way throughout this book, I will define a few words. I know you're smart; I don't question that. I define words here for context, and direction on how to use them with this book to its fullest.

Definition: Admit. Confess to be true or to be the case, typically with reluctance.

I want you to look carefully at these questions, and answer them honestly to yourself. Do it quickly, since your first gut reaction is usually your truth:

- Are you happy?
- Sleeping soundly every night?
- Having great sex when you want?
- Does your body look the way that you want?
- Do you feel right in your body, your mind?
- Are you able to chat or discuss hard topics with your partner, husband, best friend?
- Do you even know what you want?
- Are you clear about the direction of your life?
- Do you have a vision?
- Are you living by a mission statement or a clearly defined path?

- Do you have values that drive you and your decisions?

I want you to know the direction of your life, and I want you to stay on course. I know I've just rattled off a lot of questions to consider, but if you don't begin somewhere, nothing will change. Sometimes, it is challenging to admit these answers. Admitting requires you to investigate, look at, turn over rocks, and open old closet doors to discover the truth about your life. Most people are afraid to search, fearing that what they will find is beyond their imagination. Yes, imagination is exactly that—not the truth.

What I've discovered is that there comes a time in one's life when we can no longer deny what's beneath the rocks hidden deep within us. We must search fearlessly, admitting our innermost secrets about where we've been in our lives. We have to own up to who we are so we can begin to change. When we submit to change, we can show up and be the person we are meant to be in the world.

I've admitted to a lot in my life:

I eat when I'm bored.

That my life life sucked after I dropped out of school.

That I was raped by a fraternity house.

I disowned my parents several times for not being good parents.

I thought that postpartum was going to kill me.

That my marriage felt hopeless after my son was

born.

I failed as a business owner, because I no longer wanted my lingerie business.

That my belief of living on the other side of the planet would solve my problems. I've had to admit several times that I have no idea how to be a parent.

That I fallen in love with several women, and felt loads of shame.
My life doesn't work well on my own accord.

Hundreds of times admitting huge faults from quick decisions.

Too often I've found myself wandering off my own path. I then find my way back months later, kicking myself because my path, mission, or vision of my life wasn't crystal clear. I was swayed by someone or something... and it was never good!

I spent a year in Boulder, Colorado, dating the sexiest man I had ever seen and known. We had the steamiest sex I'd ever experienced, had meaningful discussions about the environment, philosophy, and world religions. We even watched football together while devouring chili-cheese fries on the couch. People thought we were a match made in heaven.

What I was omitting from our conversations, and what I ignored for that year of my life, was his alcoholism. Every night he drank—to the point of blacking out. When he was sober, yes, we had those meaningful, romantic moments, we had the best sex ever, but those moments were *few and far* between. I held my breath when he showed up at my house; I never knew whether he would be sober or three sheets to the wind.

I had to sit down and admit that this relationship didn't work... I was terrified to ADMIT that I had just spent the better part of a year in a broken relationship. Would I ever find someone else? Would I ever have orgasms like that again? Would I walk into the room and feel like a lady, like I did when I was on his arm? These questions not only betrayed me, but they kept me in the relationship while ignoring the true issue—*his drinking*. I didn't want to answer the questions, but every once in a while the truth would float to the top.

I knew in my heart that a long-term relationship could not work with someone who was drinking every day to escape *something*. I flip-flopped from being the caretaker who pitied his hangovers, to Judge Judy, who called him an asshole when he showed up on my doorstep drunk. The answer to a looming question, "Am I happy with him," frightened me deeply. I ignored it until I couldn't any longer! I look back and know that that was a year of my life I wish I could have done differently. I could have walked away months before the realization that he *wasn't* going to change, but I didn't. I stayed and watched the hours and days go by me. I worried about him, about me, about my own recovery, if I would get pregnant, if he would end up in jail. I allowed my thoughts to rob me of my life— from being present and ultimately being connected, and living with Grace.

What is more interesting is that Grace made it super clear for me to walk away without second-guessing myself. He came over one night after a business trip. He looked completely different with a shaved face, shorter hair, and bloated from one too many drinks. He told me he was going away. When I asked him where and for how long, he didn't answer me. His big beautiful eyes were now dull and heavy with what felt and seemed like regret.

He responded with, "You've been so good to me, so kind. Thank you." As he was speaking, my head filled with love and I tried to admit in that moment he was my partner in life; it felt oddly cold yet safe and warm in my heart. *Something* felt off, deep down, but I ignored it. I asked him when I would see him again, and he told me it was over. He kissed me gently, turned, and walked away from me. I never saw him again, but I tried. I went to his job. "No, he doesn't work here any longer." I went to his house and peered in the windows—everything was gone, even the Lazy Boy chair that we would fall asleep in was gone. It was as if he disappeared into thin air. For months I searched and waited for him to show up at the diner where I was slinging eggs. He was never to be seen again.

For a while, I imagined that I had dreamed him up to make it easier on my psyche. Then one day, by chance, I ran into one of his skiing friends who unknowingly gave me details of his unexpected departure. He had been taken away to serve time for a mistake he'd made one night while under the influence. I heard the news and it all made sense; everything crystallized. He had admitted to me how kind I was, which ultimately led me to my admission of simply loving him for who he was. *Admission brings freedom.*

Why we must admit.

It's simple. It's part of our Journey to Resolution. Our minds work best when there is little room for it to expand and create more stories or negativity. We are hardwired to a negative bias. This means we will create outrageous stories to prove a point or support a story. One of the main reasons I'm writing this book is to help you define your Soul's deepest desire, but first you must admit to your innermost self what it is that you're looking for. *What is it?*

Be unquestionably clear with yourself. I want you to really mull this over in your head right now. What is it that you want, now? Throughout these pages I will ask and share empowering questions with you. They are the same questions I ask my clients when they sit across from me. Empowering questions engage your brain in an unexpected way—they ask you to be present in the moment but involve a future pretense. This questioning engages your prefrontal cortex, the executive decision-making part of your brain.

What do you actually desire? Less mess, better romance, a smaller waist, hot sex, stimulating conversations, not to feel hungover, a sexy body, perfect health, a better job, nicer friends? More money, a husband who adores you, a family? To move to the other side of the country, to live on an island...? Name it, name it all.

WRITE IT DOWN NOW:

Was that exciting to let your mind admit to your Soul's desire? It's interesting what comes up when you take the time to consider and engage in what *is* possible. Now think about three years from now. What do you want? It's possible. As a result of taking a few simple steps, you can have it all—seriously!

WRITE IT DOWN NOW:

Don't forget that I'm here with you excavating the landscape and picking up rocks, looking at what's underneath each of them. I will share tools with you to uncover your way to becoming connected. (If you ever need me, remember you can always yank on my sleeve and ask for help. My email inbox is waiting for you: lane@lanekennedy.com). For additional support listen to my podcast, Your Intuition Knows on Itunes.

We all come into and go out of life the same way. Life is an equal opportunity job. It's what each of us does with it that differentiates us. Our job on this planet, during this time, is to live it fully. It's what we create—get that—you build it, how do you want your job to be? You can create the best life, when you start paying attention to details, and when you listen to your Inner Voice. You can suddenly become different; live on the edge. Become bold! Feel all of what life has to offer you. You begin to explore and take challenges even when you are not looking for them.

We, as Steve Jobs called us, are The Crazy Ones.

> *Here's to the crazy ones, the misfits, the rebels, the troublemakers, the round pegs in the square holes... the ones who see things differently— they're not fond of rules... You can quote them, disagree with them, glorify or vilify them, but the only thing you can't do is ignore them because they change things... they push the human race forward, and while some may see them as the crazy ones, we see genius, because the ones who are crazy enough to think that they can change the world, are the ones who do.* Steve Jobs

Are you a crazy one, too? I hope so.

"Forever I felt it shelter to speak to you." Emily Dickinson

CHAPTER 2
Finding Your Voice & Emotional Awareness

Everyone at some point in their lives has thought, "What the hell am I doing? Do I matter? Does this matter?" These passing thoughts are moments that rise to the top of our lives, and many times we ignore them. Then by pure chance or accident, we listen. We listen as a result of a walk in the rain after being locked out of the house, watching the birth of a child after twelve laborious hours, or as we sit in traffic on the 405 or any other Interstate, we hear it and wake up.

When we are awake, there is no turning back. We must step into this connection, or our lives become lonely and unfulfilled. Dissatisfaction settles over us, dimming our light to a small flicker. When we deny being awake and connected with the Soul's Desire, the body becomes ill and weak; we wilt and wither. In my opinion, not living a life of fulfillment affects the body-mind connection. If you were to study the heart and see how powerful this living organism truly is—I don't think you would fall victim to mistreating it.

As soon as I stepped away from my Divine Grace, I unknowingly tortured my body with a few glasses of wine every night, candy, ice cream, hot dogs, chips, mac & cheese, and anything else that wasn't pulled up from the ground (natural or organic). I let the shelves of the grocery store pollute my system. And in turn, my system broke. When I was diagnosed with Autoimmune Disorder Syndrome, there were less than 100 published studies on the immune system. No one was talking about this; no one had a clue as to why my white blood cells were attacking my body. Not even the best doctors in Beverly Hills could answer my questions.

I was broken, sick, and so far from myself, I had no choice but to seek an answer. I could have become a victim, I could have complained—but the pain was too great and my mind wouldn't rest. I dove into mystical books, herbs, potions, supplements, poop protocols, movement with flower essence, painful lymphatic massage, olive oil treatments, shamanic journeys, psychic readings, EMT, tapping (before it was a thing), and mud baths. I revamped my diet. I studied with woo-woo practitioners; I dove deep into the *Science of Mind,* with Ernest Holmes and Michael Beckwith before Agape was to become a "thing". The hunt for me to understand my purpose and know the answers to the "what the hell am I doing, do I matter" questions rose to the surface. I no longer had a choice; I was now making a decision to KNOW my purpose.

You can't be in denial of who you are, what you have to say, or what your mission is in life. Many people are in denial about who they are—are you? Are you ignoring all the signs? Ignoring the inner voice that whispers the truth? *What if you listened to that voice?* Moments continue to pass you by and you tend to ignore the whispers. I ask you, what are you ignoring?

Let's start walking towards an answer.

Here's one of the first road signs to pay attention to and gain clarity from; take a moment to write down your answers to these questions:

Take out your trusted notebook and grab a pen it's writing time. ((Or if you prefer you can jot it all here on these pages).

1. What are you continually ignoring? (e.g. pain in your body, an uneventful life, lackluster relationships)

2. What brings you so much joy today that when you're in that moment, nothing else matters—time stops, Divine Grace is present, and flow is alive within you? (e.g. traveling, writing, riding your bike to work)

3. What moves you to your deepest happiness at any given moment? (e.g. playing with your child, listening to music on a run, laughing with your girlfriends) Do you pay attention to those moments or just ignore them?

When you pay attention to these answers, you will begin to shift and connect. Your shield of self-protection collapses just enough to deeply feel your heart, and you become vulnerable with yourself. This is when you learn to become who you are meant to be. Your heart can then lead you with its brain. Yes—the heart has its own brain, rhythm, and power. It emotes to your highest self, connecting you to *Grace*. Let's find your heart!

Definition: Vulnerable. Susceptible to physical or emotional attack or harm.

Imagine for a moment if you allowed this feeling of vulnerability to reveal itself every day. What a shift in your life, your relations, your world you would have. Own your vulnerable self, it's who you are.

For the next three minutes, I want you to find your heart and get into Coherence. Are you asking, "What the heck is that, Lane?" Good question. I found Coherence when I became a High-Performance Human Potential Coach, and it was perfect timing. I was so detached from my heart I could barely take deep, connected inhales. I couldn't even feel it when I placed my hand over my chest while resting. Coherence is a rhythmic heart rate variability, bringing you into alignment. Think—super chill and relaxed! Stress levels fall, and our intuitive intelligence increases. We become *heart-centered*. Often I find my biggest "Ah-ha" moments here, client lives change here, our perception of the worst thing to happen to us suddenly becomes the best, our performance hits a peak, and we feel unique, *Grace Happens*.

We tap into greater knowing. Hold your hand to your heart and breathe into your heart slow and steady. Focusing on the power of your breath, clear your mind. Breathe out from your heart and expand. Stay with your awareness. Then, extend that awareness to love, joy, peace—breathing into and exhaling the words from your heart. Like opening and closing of an envelope, easily and gently allowing the words to drift from you into the world, extending from your heart center. As you do this, the deviation of your heart and mind find ease. Stay with it. Tap in and feel the power of your heart and *Grace*. Write down what comes up: resistance, love, joy, calm, warmth, serenity, angst—anything your body feels.

Tomorrow, I want you to use this exercise to find deeper coherence. Make sure you registered for the extras here: https://lanekennedy.com/grace-happens

Let's keep walking. Being in the world on your terms takes guts. It also takes a willingness to use your voice and speak your mind. Finding your voice and learning to listen to that voice, becoming vulnerable, getting honest, choosing acceptance, cultivating inner strength, finding your worth, and following your own path are all essential tools in walking toward your *genuine* self. Without these, you're utterly lost.

One of the most powerful actions you can take is to find and connect with your voice. While the first person you do it for is you, it's also for your family, your friends, and the world. The world needs each of us to create, inspire, and bring our best selves forward. It needs each of our unique strengths.

Before this path, I ignored the urgency of what I heard. I stayed out late, slept with people who I never would even have a conversation with, lied to people I loved, and always swore to myself that next time would be different. It was never different. I continued to drink, continued to use, continued to eat too much, continued having sex with strangers far too often, to completely disconnect and not tap into this *Intelligence*.

Finding this voice and becoming vulnerable enough to listen to it, to believe in it, to have faith in it—thus, begin to use it—allowed me to deepen my relationships—all of them. It enables Grace to happen. It also allows for community. And in community, we thrive. We need each other; we're not meant to live alone. We are creative and brilliant, and we need to share and help each other shine.

We live in a world that has become wirelessly connected. Rather, an illusion of connection. The stats reveal a different truth. More people today are suffering from isolation. Isolation leads to depression, which is at a staggering high in this day and age. Over 16 million people report experiencing depression. Meanwhile, 40 million adults in the United States are struggling with some form of anxiety. Yet only 39% of them are seeking treatment.

Imagine for a moment a group of women. They are all sitting around a table eating a meal together—sharing, telling stories, smiling, laughing, and connecting face to face. Do you think if you were sitting in this community with a supportive group, your anxiety or depression would surface? I'm going to say no, it would not. The research on being involved in a group is merely this: community feeds our emotional lives. We need each other, now more than ever.

The Truth: We are all born with this voice.

You were born with a voice innate within you. It's the voice that tells you, "I need to eat." It's the voice that guides you to drink milk from your mother. It's the voice that leads you to differentiate between right and wrong, it tells you how to show up and be in the world... right size, right-minded.

When I was at one of my last companies, working 14-hour days, ignoring my child, suffering from postpartum and barely eating, I decided to take my dog, Jackson, for a walk in the rain. I was desperately trying to zone out, but then this one word came to me. "Quit." I knew that I had heard that same voice before, and I had heard that same word before, once a long time ago. I tried to continue on my walk, but I couldn't. I went home, wrote about what I had just heard, and that's when *more* was revealed. I had given up on me and what I wanted to share with the world.

Yes, I loved lingerie. But hey, let's face it—it's not life-changing. I had begun to resent my amazing partner, the company, even the creative process. I was bitter; I knew I had to make changes. I made a list of pros and cons of taking an exit from my company. I wanted to ignore this moment. I wanted to eat, I wanted to open a bottle of my husband's finest wine, and I wanted to block out the voice of reason and truth.

Instead, I did what I knew I had to do. I called my business partner and explained to her that I could no longer partake in the business and wanted to take a formal exit or close the company. It was devastating to me and to her. I was in shock. I had worked so hard in this business, it was who I was, I needed something to prove to myself and to the world. This company *had* to be successful.

The voice came back to me and clearly explained in words on paper that I couldn't continue living in a void. I was in a black hole, trying to fill it with the rush of business and success—which was never satisfying. The illusion of self-importance was overwhelming, but I knew in my heart that if I continued, I would eventually lose what I had worked so hard to establish: my *emotional well-being*. The glue that held me together, this **connection** that I once so fondly celebrated, would be lost. I was already feeling the results of not being present with my son, my body was already aching every day. Yes, I had been miserable for months, ignoring myself and everyone else who was important to me. I am grateful that I used my words, my voice. I quit and have never looked back with regret. I actually celebrate my ex-partner's success and love that she persevered diligently through a challenging time. What an amazing woman!

So let me ask you this: Are you listening?

The Obstacle: We stop listening to this voice.

As we age and go through experiences, we lower the volume on this subtle yet powerful voice because the world becomes busier, louder, and noisier in a very distracting way. We begin to lose connection with our voice—and, therefore, our self. Instead, we connect with what we *think* other people want us to be. We strive for an "ideal" that is not real, which comes from the cultural norms— magazines, Instagram feeds, Facebook posts, peer groups, colleagues, partners, classmates, media. We lose touch with who we are, what we want, what moves us. And suddenly we feel as though we are simply going through the motions of life. We are on mute or auto-pilot and totally disconnected. Life becomes ordinary, dull, humdrum. We live to exist. Well, I believe we exist to live out our fullest heart's desire. What do you believe?

How disconnected are you?

Are you on your own path? Or have you been following a heavily trodden path, following someone else—copying, mimicking, and following a tribe you're not even sure you want to be in? You're not following the beat of your own drum. Perhaps you're not even pursuing the dream your heart desires. Instead, you're merely surviving. Are you afraid to step out, afraid of what others might say about you, afraid of falling down, afraid that you won't be able to get back up if you do fall? Are you afraid of failure?

Definition: Failure. Lack of success.

Being afraid of failure is your enemy. For a moment, I want you to remember something you have failed. It could be a job, a race, making an attempt for your team's final score, perfecting a soufflé; it could be anything you failed. After that failure, you didn't die, did you? Life went on, people around you most likely forgot and moved on in their life, but did you? Did you embed that failure into your brain into a neural pathway that has now become a failure loop? Or did it become an opportunity that you could capitalize on at a later date? Most of us embed failure. This impacts our emotional state. Our emotions are then stunted and our path, growth, dreams, desires, and connections stop! We halt the flow. Our natural abilities to accomplish and achieve our heart's desires die. I want you to connect right now to a failure—one that is looped into your conscience. Got it? Now, I want you to turn on some music, dance, laugh, recreate the circumstance with new emotion, while dancing and laughing. Let's change the negative connotation you've associated with this loop, our emotion can hold us in the past, I want you to push yourself to an uncomfortable boundary with joy and laughter with this failure. You are capable of rewiring and rewriting it as a happy memory; even though you "failed," the situation offered a learning point and opportunity for you. I hope you've been able to capitalize on your failures—this is the magic of your emotional future success. Change your future story.

What happens when we don't listen to our Inner Voice?

As we go through life's trials and tribulations, gut-wrenching breakups, terminations from jobs we loved, and heartaches of every kind, we walk along that well-worn path of others while on auto-pilot, ignoring a calling. We stop listening. Deep within, we know that if we do listen and we see that we're not on our own trail-blazing path, then there will have to be some sort of shift—a change in our direction. We will have to expend some carefully thought-out effort to bring us back to our own path. Inevitably, we will have to change something—and likely that something will be what we've been ignoring for years.

Here's an easy example from Shelly, a client of mine: "I want to break up with my boyfriend." It flashed in her mind quickly, but she completely ignored it. Why? Because if she sincerely looked at that statement, got vulnerable, listened to it, investigated it, she undoubtedly would have to move out, give up the luxury of living in a large house, and change her status.

> *Definition: Status. The relative social, professional, or other standing of someone or something.*

She sadly recognized that the life she had been building was now part of a lie that she had been ignoring. She began to hide that information from herself. She completely stopped listening to her inner voice that was shouting every day. She started to drink every day, she spaced out on TV, began shopping and spending too much money to drown out that single thought—her truth. She did whatever it took to quiet her *inner voice*.

Typically, this means hurting yourself in some way. Why? Because we don't want to know the truth. We are afraid of change. Shelly was afraid of being alone, of being single, working on herself, and finding something better... connecting with her inner source. She didn't know the power that it held. No one had ever shared with her how important that inner connection is to her life. She wasn't given a manual, and her mother never shared how to listen to her inner whisper—her powerful intuitive voice.

Eventually Shelly left, but the battle of coming back to herself was like trekking up Mount Everest with only one pack of supplies: possible but remarkably challenging. She found herself 40 pounds overweight and diagnosed with diabetes. A lot had to change, but she started off with facing her inner voice—with a little help from me. She began to listen, and her life began to evolve slowly. She dropped the weight; her diabetes fell into what I like to call a diabetic remission. She now owns a condo and is the proud owner of Henry, a yellow lab that she walks daily.

I gave Shelly exercises to change the neural pathways of a failed relationship. She had embedded that failure for months by ignoring it. I had her change her state three times per day with music. This slowly changed that pathway and her limiting belief of being a failure in her relationship (by the way, it was not a failing relationship on her part). Changing her emotional state, those neural peptides connected her to her Divine Grace.

Why we need our voice.

The importance of having a voice and having the ability to use it positions you in such a way that you become a part of the world and what's around you. If you're in the world, sitting silently and not having a point of view, you're going to be unfulfilled and not *connected* to the world around you. Do you realize that there are hundreds of people right now in your community who need to hear from you? People are desperate and want to hear from you. Listen to your inner guidance that's calling. It whispers to you every day. Pay attention. What are you holding back from everyone?

Definition: Guidance. Advice or information aimed at resolving a problem or difficulty, especially as given by someone in authority.

Finding your voice is one of the most compelling undertakings that you can explore. It's not only for yourself, but for your family, friends, and the world. Remember, finding your voice is imperative for yourself, but also for those around you. The world needs you to create, inspire, and bring your best self forward, to continue the growth we need in order for the planet to continue evolving. Your Divine calling is a part of our evolving world.

When you find your voice and know the truth, you can stand comfortably in your being. You will have a strong sense of what you're worth. I believe that you're probably worth much more than what you give yourself credit for and what you're receiving. Am I close to being right on that?

When you discover your calling, when you find your voice (perhaps even again), your life takes on a different look. You wake up and realize the thing that you do with your heart is where you find your magic! You begin to live again. You become engaged, playful, fun, alive, and suddenly people around you see you differently, but, more importantly, you see yourself and the world differently. *Where is the voice? How do we tap into it (even if again)?* It's simple. Pay attention!

Are you paying attention?

In order to hear that voice, your deep soul's calling, a desire of your will, simply stop—just long enough to notice it. *Listen.* When you start to pay attention, your voice becomes a little bit louder. It can start as small as a whisper in your dream at 2:00 in the morning. You can lean into yourself and pay attention to your thoughts when you are running, when you sit and meditate, when you're cooking your favorite meal. It's these moments when your true voice, true calling, your deep Soul can reveal itself. It's there. It *knows* everything—listen. (When you listen, *Grace Happens*).

I'm requesting that you to begin to pay attention, I'm asking that you pay attention to the small things that irritate you, things that disturb you, to those conversations that you don't want to have; pay attention to people who are bringing up issues that put you on edge. When you pay attention, you will begin to hear what you actually have an opinion about, and it's that opinion that needs to come out and be expressed. Whether it's on paper, with a friend, or just to yourself, that voice needs to be voiced and heard. This is your Soul's Desire, the Connection, Your Truth, Grace. She's always there trying to be heard. You have a responsibility to not only listen, but to share what you hear, what you know, and take action from it.

A lot can be said for acknowledging what you care about, such as the world's overpopulation—perhaps you have real concerns about people having seven babies. Perhaps you think about the color of your skin and how you don't identify with being black or white. You have clear thoughts about how men should treat women, how women should earn the same as a man, and about how Martin Luther King started a movement and saved people with one single idea—*love*. You might think a lot, (have hundreds of your own ideas) about how the education system is failing our kids, generations to come, society at large, or how politics are an extreme joke, or celebrity worship is the way of the future.

Heck, you have thousands of thoughts. You have many fragmented ideas that linger, bubble and pass through you while others stay with you, some get buried, and others are tossed out like rotten stinky cheese. Your thoughts are critical when it comes to your calling and using your voice. If you continue to choose to sit in silence, you will continue to feel overlooked, mad, frustrated, and hopeless. When you sit and consider what it is that has you on edge, or you take the time to contemplate the unthinkable, you can then begin to formulate words. When you have words, you can start talking, creating, and sharing subjects—your stance, your opinion, what matters to you. You then become the change that you've been yearning for, and the world receives that too.

I'm sure that when you have these thoughts, you also have feelings about them. You feel angry about racial comments, injustice, and combativeness. You may feel joy and bubble up with laughter when someone mentions traveling to Vietnam. These emotions play a part in your divine process and hearing your path's direction. Emotions drive us, even unknowingly.

Expression brings freedom.

Silence brings ignorance and detrimental behaviors that affect your body, mind, and soul. I've worked with hundreds of women who have felt broken from eating too much, drinking too much, or working too much to the point of illness; chronic dysfunctional ailments appear. The biggest I see is with food.

> "I ate a whole pint of Haagen-Dazs after a phone call with my mother."

> "I ended up in a blackout after going for drinks with my co-workers to commiserate the collapse of our company."

> "I smoked three cigarettes after my husband left to release the stress."

> "I have to pour myself three glasses of wine after I put the kids to bed."

These nonchalant actions are roadblocks to your deep desire, the voice that is waiting to be heard. When you take these destructive actions repeatedly, you're adding a brick to the barrier which separates you from *your* truth. You can also think of it like adding a pound of weight to your stomach every time you ignore your voice, your Deep Calling. You gain twenty pounds, then suddenly wake up and think, *How did I get fat? These jeans don't fit me anymore!*

I want you to start paying attention to any big or small *revelations* and/or ideas that simply bother you, that irk you, that piss you off. Pay attention and start looking at forming words around the *feelings* you have about these issues. It's these ideas that will lead you on a path to your *connection* and worth, and eventually, your Soul's Calling.

Grab a pen and paper—start writing.

It can be really frightening to sit down with a pen and paper and write; I understand. It can also be nerve-wracking to sit still for more than five minutes. Honestly, who wants to do that? But that's the first step in finding your connection and revealing your message and your voice. Sitting down, even five minutes at a time, will begin to change you. It's only five minutes with a pen and paper—writing down what feels necessary, writing down what your true self desires, and what your heart wants to sing about. It can be anything. It could be starting a business, getting married, having a child alone, going to Africa and serving in a tribe, writing a book, or maybe going on stage to sing and perform. What is it? There is something that your heart desires, and that is the thing that is going to propel you forward to Connection, your desire, your Soul's Calling.

If you could do anything right now, what would it be?

EXERCISE: Get quiet.

What does it feel like? Imagine yourself doing that thing. Write it out and imagine the lines in your face moving, the feeling in your stomach, the temperature of your breath—get it all out on paper!

WRITE IT DOWN:

Any path will inevitably have obstacles. Sometimes there are rocks in our way that we may have to turn over or move to the side. Facing these stumbling blocks head on and turning them into stepping stones is part of your journey.

Overturning rock number one: Recognize your voice and your dream.

Think of something you have wanted to explore, but always stopped and dreamt about it for another time... Write down that exploration. Say it out loud. Pay attention to what you are saying. Repeat. How does it feel to explore it? Imagine deeply. Listen to your heart.

Example:

I have a deep Soul Desire to explore riding in a biplane with my fiancé before we get married.

1. What holds you back from those dreams stated above?
2. Why does it hold you back? (Is this an emotional issue? Financial? Mental?)
3. When did it begin? (Middle school, high school, 5 years ago?)
4. How does the why affect your status? (Not your social status)

Definition: Status. The relative social, professional, or other standing of someone or something.

Answer these questions in regard to your desire (see example below):

1. What holds me back? (*I don't have the money.*)

2. Why does it hold me back? (*My job only pays me X amount per year.*)

3. When did it begin? (*I took the job out of total desperation. I knew that my salary would be lower than I wanted, but I needed the job. I took the job out of desperation.*)

4. **How does the why affect my status?** (I'm stuck. My

status stays small, and I feel like I'm unseen. I feel like I'm not worthy of a fun trip because I don't make enough money. I'm afraid of never being enough, and ultimately being alone in my life.)

I want you to deeply investigate your emotions with question #4. From the example above, "I'm stuck"—digging in to that statement we could find, *I'm feeling, small, unseen, not worthy, afraid, alone*—these are all super charged emotions that stop an action, or in this case, this particular exploration. These emotions deliver reality, so we always need to identify them. Once they're identified and named, we can get to the point of the cause. For now, hold this awareness: "My emotions create my reality." When we change our emotional state, we change our journey.

Now it's your turn. Let's begin connecting to your Soul's Desire and Grace. Let's co-create. Ready, Set, Go!

MY DREAM:

WHAT HOLDS ME BACK?

WHY?

WHEN DID IT BEGIN?

HOW DOES THE *WHY* AFFECT MY STATUS?

Now: What steps can you take to get your Soul's Calling? I want you to create a list of actions you can take while listening and tuning into your Soul's Calling to create your bold reality!

Example:
1. Google search for companies that provide rides.
2. Start a savings account specifically for the trip that is automatically withheld from my paycheck.
3. Research Napa for accommodations for our trip.
4. Find a freelancing gig to make extra money for our trip.
5. Look at the job market and see if there are other

opportunities out there for me.

6. Update my resume.

7. Ask friends for referrals, tell everyone that I'm looking for a job and I need help finding new opportunities.

Your turn!

Go to your notebook and write the steps that you can take to fulfill that **one** dream you wrote about. Draw a line through it with a big black Sharpie pen once all the steps are completed.

As you read this book, I want you to focus on discovering your heart's desires and what you want to co-create with me while exploring. I also want you to write down ONE concrete task that you can achieve each day on this path. I want you to make them super simple, completely doable actions you cannot fail to accomplish.

My past clients excelled with these simple, doable tasks:

1. I want to brush my teeth three times a day.

2. I want to prepare an excellent dinner.

3. I want to write a 500-word blog post once a week.

4. I want to finish the laundry, actually fold and put away immediately.

5. I want to pick up my daughter after school every day.

Again, in your notebook, write down one task you'd like to accomplish each day. Get things done, now. Don't wait!

Taking action will change your state of emotions. You

will move toward excitement if you are in alignment with what you are looking to explore. Get this—if you are not in alignment, you will not be emoting to the extent that is necessary to bring about this exploration. Make sense?

One of the many reasons I ask you to get a notebook to use in conjunction with this book is because it will help your journey tremendously. When we see what we write down, our brain literally gets triggered on finding a way to create what is written down. Research suggests that as far as our brain is concerned, it's as if we are actually doing that thing. Writing it down is like practicing the behavior. Our brain can't (really) differentiate. Take advantage of this part of your brain's activity; improve it. This area of your brain is called the Reticular Activating System, aka RAS. It's always ready, constantly searching for ways to accomplish necessary objectives and tasks.

After writing it out, read your words aloud to yourself and the universe. "This is what I've been thinking about... this is what my heart has been telling me, and I've been ignoring it." When you do this, your RAS becomes activated. When you have these tiny bite-sized conversations with yourself, you will find more clarity. This activity will lead you to your Soul's Calling, Connection, and Grace—the direction that is necessary for your life to be fulfilling. That direction is where you will find your success.

As we travel the path and turn over rocks, pay attention to the road signs and any roadblocks that appear. They are just as important as green lights. Stay focused on this single dream. This will be what pulls you towards stepping more deeply to your Soul's Calling and Desire.

You are well on your way. Achievement happens one step

at a time from reading one page at a time; you've got this, your Soul is waiting. Congratulations on getting started, thinking bigger, and feeling your heart!

"I had this dream, and I really wanted to be a star. And I was almost a monster in the way that I was really fearless with my ambitions." Lady Gaga

CHAPTER 3

Learning to Become Vulnerable and Emotionally Open

What is vulnerability? Vulnerability is a hot topic these days—but what is it? What does it mean to really be vulnerable?

I'll share part of my definition: vulnerability is having the ability to be real, and to be truly seen.

> ***Definition: Vulnerability.*** *The quality or state of being exposed to the possibility of being attacked or harmed, either physically or emotionally.*

The essence of vulnerability is living from your heart, telling the truth, willing to be uncomfortable or wrong, and letting down your guard. Vulnerability is not having to wear a hard shell of protection or body armor, or not having to live behind brick walls in isolation all the time.

Being "present" can equal vulnerability. For example, when you've just realized that you can't stop spending money on handbags. My client Isabella had this realization a few months back in one of our sessions. Actually, it wasn't only handbags; it was also shoes and clothing. She spent hundreds of dollars on her wardrobe and accessories nearly every day. One day she said to me, "Lane, I don't have anywhere to put my clothes anymore."

I asked her, "What do you mean?"

"I keep buying clothing—it actually started with handbags. I have two closets full of every designer handbag you could think of and I don't even use them." As we talked about her spending, I heard a deeper calling from her. Statements like this began to come out: "As I grew up, we were poor. My mom worked two jobs, and my dad never worked, so I didn't have a lot of clothing. I had three outfits that I rotated throughout the week."

I asked, "How did that make you feel?" She was silent for a moment and then continued with tears welling in her eyes.

"I never wanted to cause problems at home. I knew my mom worked hard, and I was grateful for the clothes that she had managed to buy for me. I was so angry with my father for never working. I would think to myself, *why don't you work so I don't have to wear the same clothes every week?* Even my shoes had holes in them. I had one pair per school year, and at the end of the year the soles would be falling off the bottom. I was terribly embarrassed. I had a classmate, Tammy Faye, a popular little girl with blonde hair and freckles who constantly taunted me with, 'Isabella's wearing that sweater again, she only has three, and it's beginning to stink.' It was a horrible time for me."

I asked Isabella to go deeper into that moment: "Isabella, what felt horrible?"

She sat there as her eyes filled with bigger tears. They were holding back what seemed like years of rainfall that had been collected and held behind a corroded wall, ready to break at any moment. I could tell she was steps away from a breakthrough.

"I couldn't understand why my dad never worked. I was so proud of my mom for working every day—she did everything. I never wanted to let her down; she never let me down. It was my dad who was a big disappointment." Tears fell from her eyes.

"He started drinking the moment I got home from school, he woke up drunk, the house was a mess with him in it, I couldn't stand him! I still can't believe we lived like that for most of my childhood. We constantly put the house back together every day. He would yell at me, and I'd have to go to my room. That's when my closet situation began. I would take out my clothing, and try to make different outfits with the three sweaters, three shirts, three skirts, and three dresses. I wanted to fit in with everyone. All the girls had beautiful Easter dresses for spring, they had warm festive sweaters for Thanksgiving and Christmas, but I walked around with the same three outfits that my mom bought me at the beginning of the school year from Kmart. Do you know what that does to a little girl?"

I stopped her, and said yes with a small smile, "It sends an adult on endless shopping sprees."

"But that's not everything," she continued. "I was completely embarrassed with my clothing. When I finally got out of the house and began earning my own money, I would spend almost my entire paycheck every month on new clothing. This is not a new habit; I've been spending for years now."

"Would you like to stop?" I asked her.

She looked at me and silently nodded her head yes, then followed with this reaction: "I don't want to be living in the past anymore. It seems like I will never get Tammy Faye out of my head. She is always there, haunting me, and I feel hopeless, and angry at times and whatever I buy is not enough."

BINGO! We got there. Isabella started crying more. She finally allowed herself to feel her connection to anger, which was accompanied by feelings of loss, and sadness, yet at the bottom of this pool of tears was disappointment. She finally found her reason for shopping. It was the disappointment with her father, who never worked, who wasn't available as a father or as someone she could trust. Often we overlook these obvious bad habits in the important, influential people in our lives. I mean, who wants to reveal the pain of their childhood? No one, unless it means breaking a lifelong habit and entering into a personal freedom that you can only learn of after the fact. This is terrifying to most. Stopping and listening to your inner voice, and revealing it, can feel like 35 seconds of the earth's tectonic plates shifting in your own backyard; it's terrifying! You feel like you might never stop crying.

Isabella's tears didn't stop for three weeks. We worked diligently, excavating the events of her sixth grade. We found that to be the year when Tammy Faye and her crew of friends really created the biggest impact. It was also the year that Isabella's dad was put into jail for drunk driving. She uncovered thirty years of disappointment, shame, embarrassment, and fear in three sessions. Her handbag shopping sprees came to a screeching halt, along with her clothing binges. She stopped spending money haphazardly and was able to start saving money to put into a retirement plan.

Here I'm going to point out a term I use, the *hammered* emotions. Isabella lived day in and day out with emotions that trapped her progress, they hammered her daily. She was in a loop of self-destruction from her deep essence of not having enough. It was embedded when she was eight, the first time her father didn't show up for her birthday. Her ability to co-create positive habits weren't possible — she had no fruitful, happy emotions with growing up, she was stuck, together we released, revived and rewired her neural pathways.

Vulnerability allows you to be seen, heard, and held. Vulnerability changes you from the inside out.

Being "real" means different things to different people. Recently I was told by a very good friend that I remind her of Brené Brown. This got under my skin a bit because I don't wish to be compared to anyone else. I'm not one to seek and read self-help books, and when I've done so in my past, they've been books from Buddhist monks or spiritual seekers from decades or centuries ago. Needless to say, I was not that familiar with Brené's work. My friend's statement had me curious, so what does my curious mind do? I typed into Google, "Brené Brown." I took a moment to read up on Brené and how she defines vulnerability. After all, she is someone in the world who has done a significant amount of research and has one of the most viewed Ted talks on the subject. Here are some of Brené's highlights: "...The way to live is with vulnerability and to stop controlling and predicting. Vulnerability is also the birthplace of joy, of creativity, of belonging, of love..." After reading a bit from Brené, I could see where she was going and became okay with being compared to her.

Having the ability to be vulnerable with oneself is where this work of finding your true self and Connection or Your Soul's Calling begins. If you are able to look yourself in the eye—yes literally in a mirror—and not pretend to be someone else, or hide from yourself, you can begin to be vulnerable with other people, too. Being available and vulnerable with someone else is magical. How often are you available?

What's behind vulnerability? Courage.

Definition: Courage. The ability to do something that frightens one.

The courage to risk being rejected for what you stand for, your dreams, and your truth—not shape-shifting according to your surroundings so other people will like you (aka being a "people-pleaser") is a *big* deal. People-pleasers aren't able to be vulnerable, are they? They're always seeking approval from others, which can also lead them to sacrifice their own values, their emotions, inner calling and inner voice.

I want to introduce you to my client Amy, single, bright, and ambitious, she owned her own successful company, and traveled extensively for months at a time. From the outside looking in, she had it all—a beautiful house she bought with her own capital; her company was recognized and had won awards in her industry; she drove a luxury car; traveled the world; and drank cappuccinos at bistro tables on the streets of Paris. It was a picturesque life. You could frame it and hang it on the wall, and that's what she did. Her photo collection was amazing. During one of her routine trips to Paris, she met a woman who she was immediately attracted to—as in sexual chemistry was sparked.

Mind you, Amy's entire dating life up to that point had been with men. She had never been with a woman. When she encountered Bridget, she knew something was different. She ignored Bridget's genuine interest and candid invitation to explore Paris. She ignored her because deep within her lived fear of the unknown. Amy reached out to me to ask me what I thought was going on with her and her feelings.

"Lane, I've never been attracted to a woman. I don't understand it, but every time I'm within one hundred feet of the cafe where Bridget works, my skin feels different, my heart seems lighter, and I'm afraid. I'm afraid. What's going on with me, what's wrong with me?"

As I listened to Amy, I could sense that her very thick external layer of protection that was once on her body felt like she had taken it off and forgot where she placed it. "Amy, why not explore friendship with Bridget? You don't really know what her intentions are, and you certainly don't know how the two of you will get along after one tour of the city sipping coffees." She was silent. "If it goes horribly wrong, you never have to see her again, but what if you actually enjoy her company? And guess what it doesn't have to mean you're gay or even become a sexual relationship."

Amy agreed to meet up with Bridget and explore Paris—one cafe at a time. Amy arrived at the cafe, nervous yet willing, excited, dressed in a new dress she'd bought recently at the Open Air Market. She was wearing her best shoes and had gotten her hair done. Her nerves on fire, she sat down and waited for Bridget. I'm going to let you read a letter she sent me that shows how she found her way to vulnerability. (I'm sharing this with her permission, of course).

When Bridget sat down in front of me and she said hello, my heart sank and the world stopped. I have never felt like this with anyone before, it was as if I was sitting naked in front of her but it wasn't strange or shameful. It was actually a sense of relief. She made a joke as soon as she sat down, effortlessly breaking the unspoken tension. I'm quite sure she felt it too. We drank our first cappuccino and she offered me a cigarette, of which I don't smoke but in this minute I took it and inhaled deeply. I should have known at that moment I was breaking my own values because I wanted to please her, I wanted her to like me, so we smoked together. I wanted her to think I was just as glamorous as she was. I desperately wanted her to acknowledge me and understand me. All of this was unspoken.

That first cigarette led me to two hours, then days, then weeks of behaviors that I didn't even know I had in me. I spent three months with Bridget at her beck and call, waiting on her hand and foot, and ultimately losing my identity. She seduced me with her eyes, her words, and her body. I became powerless over this woman. My need to please her became expensive. One day I bought an entire flower shop of roses. I paid her rent, we ate lavish meals and took weekend trips to the countryside. In a matter of three months I was in love—at least I thought it was love. I told her my every thought; completely opened myself to her.

I received news from my assistant that there was a rather large job back home in the States. I knew I had to leave, but I wanted Bridget to come with me and wanted her by my side. I told her I'd pay for everything, all she'd have to do was get her visa together.

My assistant had already forwarded me the information to give Bridget regarding her visa. It was easy and could all be done in a week. Bridget said no. I was devastated and couldn't understand. She had no answer, no response to my questioning. I told my assistant to cancel the job and I stayed in Paris with Bridget. I bought us a pair of tickets to Amsterdam. She always talked about the city and how I would love it. I wanted to surprise her. When she came home, I had the tickets in an envelope on the dining table with a vase full of lilacs. I was so excited to share the good news, but it was interrupted with a distant sense of dissatisfaction. Bridget was angry.

Lane, I wanted to grab the tickets, run, and never go back. I could tell something was wrong. She started yelling at me in French. I had little understanding of what she was saying, then she said it in English loud and clear: "I'm leaving!" She went into the bedroom and started throwing her clothes into her orange case.

"Where are you going? What's wrong? Please let's talk about this," I said. She said nothing and continued to pack her belongings. "Bridget, what have I done, will you please tell me?" I

wanted her to explain why she had settled on leaving. Had I not given her everything? Wasn't I the dream she had explained to me? Lane, I am so confused.

Bridget packed her bags and left that night and I haven't seen her since. It's been 3 weeks. My assistant, Cheryl, finally persuaded me to come home. I'm leaving Paris on Thursday and should be back at my house in my bed Friday night. Needless to say, I'd like to see you to get my head straight when I return. When can I see you?

When I received Amy's letter, I cleared time for a session for the week of her return. Meanwhile I quickly responded:

"Amy, I'm looking forward to seeing you. It's been a long time and I've missed you. In order for us to get the most from our time together, I would like you to do a little homework. Make sure you bring it with you when I see you next. Please take your time to sincerely answer the following questions after you tap into your own happiness, do not waiver with your emotional state when you begin this assignment:

1. *Make a list of everything you did for Bridget.*
2. *What did you sacrifice, if anything, for your relationship with Bridget?*
3. *What expectations were never met?*
4. *When did the expectations begin?*
5. *What are you afraid of?"*

When Amy and I had our session, she was armed with her homework.

"It's been a long time, Amy." I said as we sat together.

"I know." She said while looking down at her sneakers.

She looked exhausted. Her eyes were bloodshot. Her normally short sassy haircut was grown out, leaving her looking like a burnout—not the successful professional I knew her as before. I had my work cut out for me.

With knowing everything I did about Amy, I jumped in with my first question and what she had written to me about Bridget.

"How's your spiritual practice?" I knew the answer, but in order for her to uncover herself, I had to back up a bit and ask a relatively simple question. Her response was exactly what I expected.

"It's non-existent, unless you count my spinning classes." I smiled at her and shook my head, *no*.

"Are you ready to let go of being a people-pleaser?"

She shrugged her shoulders. "What are you saying? Me? A people pleaser I am not."

"Seems like this woman has pulled your last string. You can't please her, you couldn't change her mind, buy her, or get her on the plane. You can't make someone love you, want you, like you when you constantly try to please them, buy them, give to them. External forces only go skin deep. It's the internal emotions people fall in love with and, more importantly, respect."

"But I thought it was going great. We had the best sex I've ever had in my life. For Christ's sake, I changed everything for this woman—something I never even knew I could do or wanted to do."

She noticed my eyebrow raised.

"I guess I'd fantasized, but my parents would have disowned me if I came home for the holidays with a girlfriend. It was better not to stir up the drama at my parent's house, especially with all the chaos of my younger sister."

"Was your relationship based solely on sex, Amy?"

"No. Yes. No. We did a lot of fun things the first month and I bought her lots of gifts, lavish extreme outfits. I couldn't help myself—beautiful lingerie, flowers, jewelry. I even paid her rent."

"Amy, when did you know it was not going the way you planned?"

"I didn't know—until she said no."

I raised my brow again, questioning her without saying anything.

"Actually about a month ago she came home late and my stomach immediately tied into knots, but I couldn't put my finger on it. After that night everything seemed to change. Whatever I did wasn't enough for her. My ideas, jokes, even breakfast in bed wasn't enough. It felt like she had moved on but was still there physically. I thought this trip to Amsterdam would bring us together. I was so wrong."

Amy eventually got over Bridget and learned how to give without breaking her own values or going against her beliefs. Amy slowly learned how to connect and stand up for her beliefs and understand that giving doesn't have to compromise her feelings or her bank account. She also realized that her stomach, which tied into knots was a moment of her Connection speaking to her, *Grace* reaching through to her.

Amy and I had about three sessions before she realized that her deep desire to give came from the absence of her own mother. When she was growing up, her mother left for five years. Since then, her parents had gotten back together, but Amy realized that she always felt like she had to give and please everyone in order for everything to be okay. She believed that when she gave, people would appreciate her and accept her. Deep down within her, Amy believed that her mother left her and she chased this idea of pleasing people so they wouldn't ever leave her like her mother did.

My sessions with Amy revolved around vulnerability and values. When you are not in alignment with your values, your vulnerability and choices become compromised. As Amy fell further and further from her deep desire and her truth, her world became smaller, eventually alone in Paris.

Are you chasing an old idea? Are you confident with where you're at in the world and not trying to please everyone around you so they don't leave you, or so they continue to like you and love you? You are enough. I believe you are more than enough; you're perfect.

> **The Truth: We all have the ability to be vulnerable. It's a choice to live this way.**

Somewhere along your path, you may have gotten the idea that vulnerability is too scary, too risky. It won't work for you. That it's simply "not an option." Either with certain people (a parent, a sibling, a co-worker or boss) or in situations (in your marriage, at work, at the gym, with the other people on the school board). So you stopped trying. You may even have begun to lose touch with your own sense of who you are, what you want, and what is bothering you. All of this goes back to finding your voice, this deep connection, your divine truth. Once we find our voice, we have to be willing to use it, and share it.

You'll have to be prepared to share it again and again and again. After experimenting and using it time and again, it becomes your only way of life and going "back"—back to hiding, back to lying, back to being small, or avoiding yourself—is no longer an option. You will have to live on the edge, because going back to silence will be brutal and painful. Your body will ache, your mind will race, and your thoughts will be unclear.

The truth is, if you're not willing to listen and find your connection, your inner voice and get vulnerable without breaking promises to yourself, you're simply not going to experience life in full Technicolor. You're going to miss out on huge chunks of adventures with joy, intimacy, personal growth, inner peace, and living the life you dream of living. The truth is: not being vulnerable means living a life half lived. Who wants to live like that? Do you?

The Obstacles: Risk averse and afraid of change.

How often do you face the risk of being rejected for your ideas, big dreams, and what you stand for? What happens when what you want actually may be in conflict with your current set of life circumstances—a great looking marriage from the outside, a high paying salary at a Fortune 500 company?

Another client, Jody, works for a high profile company; a dream position that people search for and hope to acquire after years of "hard" work. When we landed on her third call with me, she said, "Lane, I can't take it anymore. The travel, the hotels, and the time away from my kids is killing me. I want to run away from my company and never go back. I want to be a mom, play with my kids, and go to PTA meetings."

I said, "Jody, what's stopping you from leaving?"

"My husband, my colleagues, my circle of friends, all of it, they look at me as success and I have to keep up with it all. I don't even have time to attend my son's first play. I'll be sleeping in a hotel room in Dallas. I don't want my life anymore. I worked so hard to get here and now I can't stand it."

I hear this story and so many just like it all the time. Our lives are a struggle. We either fear losing something we have or we are exhausted from fighting for something we think we should have. In both cases we lose.

Staying in a broken marriage, or in a job that is slowly breaking you into a thousand tiny pieces, while turning you into what everyone else wants you to be, is a slow and painful way to age. It's a slow and painful death. Breaking contact with your true deepest desire, this calling, your connection with Grace brings pounds of misery (both literally and figuratively). I have had clients lose weight overnight when they have taken a stand, listened, and leaned into their deep desire and felt confident with their Connection.

Continuing to agree with how everyone around you sees you—instead of speaking up about how you feel—is life threatening! You may think you're safe in hiding. You may believe that you're not rocking the boat, or having to face conflict. But all that energy that is being tucked away—ever so neatly just so you can play it safe—is only eating away at you. That is keeping you unhealthy, numb, overweight, underweight, sleepless, depressed, anxious, miserable, and in pain. It's time to break from it.

EXERCISE: Get quiet.

Uncovering the second rock: Finding Grace, it's a journey to *Living Fearlessly.*

It was easy to move the first rock on the path, wasn't it? Thinking bigger, searching for your voice, and finding that deep sense of Connection, your Soul's deep desire isn't everyone's first choice. For some of us it's natural, but for most others, it takes practice. A lot of practice.

As we look under our second rock, we will use a bit of creativity as your guide.

You'll be creating a Vision Quest from your Soul's Desire! Your action steps include reflecting and collecting the material that is needed for this creation. Before we begin, I want you to write down your thoughts of what your life is about and where you want it to be heading. Over the next 12 to 36 months, as you do this, your prefrontal cortex will be more open to any new ideas, images, and words as they appear while you search in your collection of magazines.

Think about your life, what you want, how you want to

live, and most importantly, how you want to *BE* in your life. Remember, vulnerability is key, and will only bring you closer to the truth. The more we can activate the RAS that I spoke of earlier, the quicker your results will begin to manifest. We are in the midst of changing your frequency, your vibration and awareness—stay with me!

Simple instructions on co-creating a Vision Quest:

Collect images from old magazines (*Vogue, Travel & Leisure, Dwell, Oprah, Elle,* whatever you have hanging around the house, old copies of *National Geographic, Parenting*).

Set your mind on an intention of feeling a particular way, choose from being happy, adventuresome, mysterious, calm, abundant, peaceful... you choose your emotional state. This is extremely important as you create.

Get your scissors.

Cut out images, words, and anything else that may inspire your vision of the world you desire.

Get a piece of construction paper or old cardboard (something to place all of your images on). Use a glue stick to paste your pictures on the construction paper. If you don't have one, get one. It's the easiest to use, trust me!

Once you've completed your Vision Quest, place it up on your wall, in a location where you are able to take a moment every day and reflect on your ideas. Get busy. This exercise is meant to be fun, so don't skip it!

Like the exercise in *"Finding Your Voice"* (Chapter 2), you're going to find discipline and begin writing things down that will move you forward. Even if you're not ready to become fully vulnerable, writing down how you feel, what you think about, and what you (really) want is powerful and contagious. Once you start, you can't stop. It becomes more challenging to ignore the truth about your desires, life, and how your deep Soul Calling reveals itself.

After your Vision Quest has been completed, the second part of this exercise includes writing the answers to the following questions in your notebook. Every day, vulnerability has an opportunity to shift when you take time to answer these questions. Every day, you'll be able to track your contact with yourself. Have fun with this. Bring joy, (or your chosen emotional unwavering state) with you into this exercise. Remember to do this every day—and get accountable with it on my Facebook page (https://www.facebook.com/lanekennedy) at least once a week to let me (and the Universe!) know.

Here are questions/prompts and example answers to get you started:

What do I want today? (I want to feel happy today! Bring on the happiness.)

What do I need more of today? (I need more time. I need more fiber in my diet.)

What am I feeling today? (I am so excited. I feel well rested.)

Why am I feeling this way? (It's not raining outside and I slept with earplugs.)

What do I desire right now? (I'd love to complete my accounting project at the office and a glass of green juice.)

What is standing in my way right now? (My boss who has an unrealistic timeline in standing in my way. I'm too lazy to stop at the store for juice.)

How do I move forward with whatever is standing in the way right now? (Ask my boss to consider timeline, show details of project and progress. Ask my partner to help me with getting more juice in the house.)

If you work toward greater accountability, your life will change—watch. Take daily action, copy these prompts into your notebook, and use them every day.

Stay with yourself as you watch what unfolds every day, plug into answering these questions, and stare into your vision board imagining each moment of your true desires. Let your mind work for you, positively. Remember the brain is always wiring and firing, working, why not set it up to collect, wire and fire to create a beautiful future?

"Freedom lies in being bold." Robert Frost

CHAPTER 4

Getting Honest with Yourself

As I touched on earlier, being vulnerable is not easy. Being vulnerable can trigger our wounds, fears, self-protection mechanisms and yes, even our worst behaviors. I've never met a single person who represents perfection in regards to being vulnerable.

Being vulnerable falls next to the principle of being honest. Self-discovery is one of the most important (and most overlooked) means to happiness. We often avoid self-searching, fearing we'll discover that we're wrong, or inadequate in some way or, worse yet, we are stricken with a deep-seated fear that we'll never reveal. A fear that perhaps after doing an exhaustive search, we discover that our way or our thoughts don't even matter. We fear that we will be discovered as a fraud—not smart enough, good enough, or bright enough—even though we have the degree hanging on the wall, or a career that pays us well, or a house in the perfect neighborhood.

The default mode of our brain does not look for happiness.

It defaults to protection and ease. We're operating from a limbic system that desperately tries to run the show. It doesn't want to expend more energy than necessary, it looks for routines and loops—even if that routine is filled with self-doubt and monotony. Thank goodness we have the prefrontal cortex that regulates and attempts to balance us by offering clear supportive instructions. Although too often, we ignore it.

Every day after dropping my son off at school, I'd come home to walk *Jackson*, my pooch. I had been doing this for almost fifteen years. He was my first "real" commitment. We hit the road rain or shine, even snow when I lived in Colorado. He looked forward to it. I craved our time together as much as he did. We used to walk out in the Presidio, a stunning National Park here in San Francisco. The path there is full of fragrant eucalyptus trees, it is soothing to the mind. Sometimes the rain would fall on us, or the fog settled over us, and we'd walk in silence on a leafy footpath. Space would often open in my heart and I'd feel safe, open, free, and vulnerable to ideas that would pop inside my brain. They'd flow in and out and I'd let them pass like hot air balloons at a fall festival. It was a magical experience.

After those walks I'd feel electric, happy, and life felt *easy*. Phone calls would come in with answers. I'd meet people on the trail with big smiles; I'd gain insight into big challenges. I often felt life was uncomplicated.

At some point, a series of events occurred in the mornings, leading me to miss this time with Jackson. Our "special" walk time was replaced with client calls and errands to the grocery store. I completely ignored my inner need for this period of solitude. Meanwhile, Jackson seemed to be getting a bit thick around the middle, which I ignored. During this "break," I began to feel more anxious and depressed. However, in my mind, I thought that taking the break from our walk was allowing me more time; offering me a more flexible schedule to "get things done!"

My brain was *betraying* me. I didn't need more time to get things done. When I'm running around micro-managing the details of life that need to be sorted out, my brain begins chasing chaos. It sends me to the grocery store even when I don't need anything in the hopes of creating a new routine—which it succeeded in doing. There's definitely no vulnerability in selecting avocados! On one of those trips to the market, I realized that the only reason I was heading to the grocery store was so that I could sip coffee and not do what was on my agenda. My agenda held one word: write. *WRITE*. Everything inside me fought the sense of ease that occurred when I was out with Jackson. My state of mind had changed, and ease had *left the room* and my body.

The routine—or loop—of mental chaos wins if I'm not actively listening and participating with my inner voice and seeking my Soul's Desire. *Connection*. I had to make a conscious decision to get myself and Jackson back outside. It wasn't easy, but I made it. This struggle lasted for months, but eventually I made it out from the daily grocery run and calls. I committed to 30 days of pen to paper. My brain literally would freeze every time I sat down to write. I would end up doodling for 30 minutes and then get up, distract myself with a cup of mushroom tea. I'd find myself back at my desk, angry. *Emotion*. I finally realized that I was stuck. Anger is such a powerful tool to wake oneself up too. I settled back into my work and wrote, rediscovered why anger was showing itself and again, asked to connect to *Grace*.

The Obstacle: Being honest with oneself is a challenging act.

We constantly lie to ourselves to fit in, feel comfortable, and not ruffle anyone's feathers. Years ago, when I was at one of the startups I was consulting with, I completely lost my ability to be vulnerable and listen to my divine sense. The CEO of the company and I got along famously, but the CFO and I did not see eye to eye. We didn't agree on anything, and we had very different points of view; different morals. My lie began when I ignored his first gesture at me —I excused his bad behavior. After our initial meeting, he neglected to say, "Pleased to meet you," and he neglected to shake my hand. This may seem trivial, but when doing business and upon first meeting someone, this is simply good manners. It's good business. The lie began when I told myself that his forgetfulness and lack of good behavior was okay and excusable.

My dishonesty continued as I told myself I would only be there for six months of work. They were paying me an extraordinary amount of money for what I was doing, and I loved it. Essentially, it was a *cash cow*. For the most part, I had gotten the company up and running, earning half a million dollars in less than a year. I considered my job safe, as well as the company; it was a smooth-rolling cash machine. My ROI was worth it (or so I thought).

My lack of honesty led me down a path that kept me away from myself. I ended up compromising my values and my vision. In the end, when I did finally leave, I wasn't happy at all, but rather further from myself than when I started the job. The truth was that I had no business working with a man whose values were completely opposite of mine. I neglected myself by not listening to my own truth. I didn't trust my inner voice. I told myself every day that it would be okay, that it would be different and, by me being there, he might see the light; he might change. *He never did.*

Some things never change, and he's still an asshole, but he taught me an important lesson: *to listen.* Even when I'm not ready to listen. It's the same lesson to pay attention to my inner wisdom, to my truth. The final coin that broke my bank of self-neglect happened when we were in a room full of colleagues and my staff. I was presenting a new program and new ideas on marketing that program. He stood up, in front of everyone, and told me to sit down. He said he wasn't interested in hearing any more from me, or about the strategy that I had created—the one that was working and generating high five-figure months which had already brought the company to a million dollars. No, he was done with me. The room was silent. I was furious, anger shot through me like a stiff shot of vodka, and I wanted to strike. Fortunately, there was a pause; my Soul's Calling stepped in and kept my tongue from taking revenge. Instead, I responded with, "Excuse me?"

He quickly replied, "We're not doing it that way anymore, sit down." I looked around the room while all eyes were on me. I swallowed hard then smiled at everyone, stepped back, and walked to my office to collect my belongings. I was done. At that moment, I listened to what I felt inside deep within me. My inner voice, which had been just a whisper, was now screaming, "LEAVE RIGHT NOW!"

Driving home that afternoon, I could clearly see the neglect I had placed on myself. I saw where my reasoning had gone awry and how I thought working 14 hours a day was the "right" thing to do. Having my cell phone attached to my hand all day and all night—going to bed with my phone—surely would prove that I was one of them. Losing touch with being vulnerable and my truth, my deepest desires, placed me in a position of working beyond my values and becoming someone else. Ultimately, I became a pawn in someone else's game. I never want to be a figure in someone else's board game, and I don't want you to be either. We are here to co-create, celebrate life, not to be under anyone's thumb!

I am grateful I sunk low enough to see the underside of the truth. The truth was I was afraid to leave a "cash cow," afraid that I wouldn't find another consulting gig like this one. I was afraid that I would lose touch with all my employees; I was afraid that I wouldn't be liked. The truth was, I didn't trust the process of letting go until that very moment when I was humiliated. I've had clients come to me and share very similar stories of being asked to compromise their values, at work, in their family, even in relations with their partners. It's this small-yet-large act of compromise that eliminates the truth from us. It sets us back and away from being Connected to our Soul's Calling, leaving us empty—there's no truth.

Finding honesty.

I ran into my girlfriend Mary at the park one day. She didn't look quite right, so what does any good friend do? I inquired, "Mary, are you okay?"

She stared at me for a moment and then burst out like a high-voltage outlet with a surge of electricity, "Lane, I want to have a baby, but I keep having miscarriages." Mary was in her mid-thirties, beautiful, worked a lot, traveled the world, and had a wonderful partner. I asked what her doctor had said, and she mentioned that all was normal, all of her labs were on target, and she *should* be able to carry a child.

Because I do the work I do, I'm invited into the private lives of many women who are trying to conceive and for one reason or another, conventional wisdom and medicine don't prevail. I then step in to help with fertility and options. I am not saying I'm some baby maker or specialize in fertility—I'm only sharing that I've been privy to several women who now have babies after working with me. But let me get back to Mary, as that's my main point here, and what I want to help you understand.

Mary's dishonesty was getting in the way of her happiness. As with several of my clients, dishonesty reveals itself through omission—self-omission. Mary had gotten a promotion a year before this conversation. Since that promotion, her life had turned upside down with mega responsibility. She was now traveling back and forth to New York every eight weeks to work in a showroom. She had numbers that she *had* to "make" every quarter. She also had taken on a new golden retriever puppy. Oh, and she was a docent at one of the museums in the city, where she gave tours on the weekends she was in town. She lived for that commitment. Her undergraduate work had been in art history—it was her first love.

Now, let me ask you: Do you think she slept at night? Do you think she took care of herself? Do you think she ever met up with her girlfriends? Would you think she was heading to the gym every day and taking care of herself, eating organic food, and meditating every day to manage her stress?

If you answered NO, then bravo, you can clearly see how crazy her life was. Yet she didn't. She could not see the unraveling of her being. She was constantly on the go—not taking care of the vessel that was supposed to hold and support a baby. Mary was blinded by her life and society's desires so much that she neglected what needed to be cared for; our bodies always know.

Our bodies are wisdom factories. They are more than two moving legs, a stomach, eyes, and some arms. This body we live in holds the memories of every macro and micro activity; it tracks each move non selectively, and it is cataloging and storing away information for (future) reference. Mary was storing the stress, the headache, and the angst in the cells of her body. She was secretly lying to herself. She wasn't *ready* for a baby. She wanted a career, she wanted to succeed, she wanted to be loved. I also want to share that Mary's partner, a wonderful human being, was also extremely busy. Working fifty plus hours a week, he unknowingly left Mary to feel isolated, alone most nights (hence the puppy). Mary could not bear the truth. She fought the voice in her head that told her she had to slow down, that she needed to speak with her partner about how she felt, and how her body was not cooperating every month. Omission is tricky.

That day when she broke down and fell into my arms, I held her. "Mary, do you think it's time to give up and start doing things differently? Are you ready to slow down and try to take care of yourself?"

She sobbed in my arms. I continued to hold her. As I held her, I felt years of grief, and then she stopped, pulled back a bit from me, but not too much and whispered, "What do I have to do, Lane, tell me."

I held her more tightly and softly said, "Stop doing so much and start being you. Slow down and allow your body to be cared for, take time off, let go of the mountain of MUST."

She let go of me a bit and said, "I don't know how; this is who I am, what I do. I'm on constantly." She took a small breath then whispered the four magic words, "Can you help me?"

Connection. As I held her, I felt the magic of connection appear. I'm not one for speaking of magic, but that is all I can equate it to. Pure energy. This connection and what I call Grace is magical. One minute she was hopeless—the next, ready to change. She was more powerful than before, more committed to her journey. I'm not sure that we can control this knowing of when we are linked up to our Soul's Calling or feeling Connection, but I do know that when we are ready it is always there. Mary began co-creating that day. She connected with her divine truth and stopped doing so much. She began her journey into *being*.

The subtle lies we tell ourselves.

You may not think that any of the following statements qualify as lying, but denial of listening to your inner voice, your Soul's Calling, is precisely that. These subtle lies—which are still lies—corrode all areas of our life.

Let's review a few, maybe you'll relate to one:

> I'm just going to wear sweatpants... because at some point I will go to the gym today, *maybe*.
>
> I've already had to glasses of wine, one more is not going to hurt anyone.

I don't have time to play with my kids... I have to do the laundry, *no one else is going to do it.*

I'm going to stop at Starbucks if there is a parking spot in front and grab a latte, even though I've had three cups of coffee today.

I missed another doctor's appointment, I *can't afford* it, yet each day my mood swings get worse!

I don't have *enough* time to eat. Meanwhile, I eat something quick, refined, and unhealthy, which makes me feel worse later.

Truth.

The truth is... we do have the capacity to be vulnerable with ourselves and others.

We have plenty of time to feel better about our lives, look better, and pay attention to what surrounds us, and what is within us. We can do challenging things. We can climb mountains and move across the country or world. We can kick ass—seriously. We can do what we set our minds to do. We simply have to begin with being honest with ourselves, reaching deep within, and connecting to our vulnerability, our Soul's Desire, and saying yes to the Universe!

EXERCISE: Get quiet.

Steady yourself with rock number three: Taking it All in

slowly.

Look back at your life and write down three times you were honest—I mean as in *DEAD* honest. No white lie, no fibbing, no stories or fabricating any of it; these moments can be about anything. Then write down what came as a result of you being honest. Were you punished (as a kid, perhaps)? Did someone tell you how great you were for returning the money you found in the bowling alley? Did you lose your best friend when you told her you didn't like her new boyfriend and that she was never around anymore? Then reflect with these questions, record what comes to you in your notebook.

- When you were honest, did it have a positive or negative outcome in your mind and in your life?
- How do you feel about being honest/telling the truth?
- Were you hopeful with your honest action(s)?
- How do you feel about the result(s) of your honesty?

Now, name three times when **you** were dishonest.

Did you copy a paper and get a good grade? Did you feel guilty about it? Did you hurt someone and ignore them? Did you hit someone's car while driving a little tipsy and not leave a note? Did you tell your kids that you had to work late when in reality you were out with your boss and colleagues for happy hour? Reflect with the same questions above using dishonesty, and record your answers. What are the differences, if any between you being honesty and you being dishonest?

Can you identify the difference in your statements and

your varied levels of honesty? If not yet, it's okay. We have a lot more to uncover, don't worry. But if you can see the subtle moments of truth, take hold and say, "Thank you," your deep Soul is revealing. Let's keep searching.

Practice: Vulnerability Part 1

For the next several days, tell yourself the truth about one thing per day. Start small. Begin with the most obvious and in-front-of-your-face facts, for instance, "I'm drinking a cup of tea right now and I don't like the bitter taste or the smell of it." Perhaps you've been drinking the tea every day because your fiancé got it for you for your birthday!

As you do this, a small critical or judgmental voice may appear, remind her, this soft voice, that this is *practice*. All we want to do is *begin* to identify the truth. I want to train you how to hear, know, and *feel* the facts of your life. Your *truth* has the same matter-of-fact tone as, "I am drinking a cup of coffee right now." Even though it may feel scary to say out it loud, or it may have an effect on you, it's really a neutral statement of what is. And it is also something you can prove, like "the flower vase on the counter is empty." It is a *fact* that you can see it sitting there, without flowers. Don't overthink this next simple exercise!

Examples:

Day 1: I am drinking a cup of coffee, it's too sweet.

Day 2: I am walking my dog, I love him.

Day 3: I am going to the gym to see my trainer.

Day 4: I am sitting in traffic and listening to music.
Practice: Vulnerability Part 2

By about Day 5, start adding some details about the facts or actions that you're doing, thinking, or feeling. How is it making you feel? What are your thoughts about it? What is happening in your body? Here is what the next five days would look like:

> Day 5: I am getting a manicure. The manicurist is being sloppy. I'm uncomfortable asking her to do my toes over again.
>
> Day 6: I can't stand eating the same salad every day for lunch. My stomach is never full and I'm still hungry, which leaves me feeling like a failure on my diet because I grab at a snack later.
>
> Day 7: I wish my husband would offer some emotional support. I need a break, and the kids are driving me crazy. I'm afraid to ask for too much. I don't feel like telling him. I'm afraid to tell him.
>
> Day 8: Making this phone call to my colleague is making me really nervous right now. My body is trembling and I'm losing my voice. I am afraid he's going to say no to my question.
>
> Day 9: These Sunday-night mastermind groups actually leave me feeling depleted and spent. I need to quit them, but I don't want to lose these relationships.

Keep going in this regard, adding as much detail as you want, and getting to Day 30. As you practice, remember that it's critical for this exercise to not be about judgment. You're only tuning in and recognizing your voice, your truth, your Soul's Calling. Honesty, is a golden key that unlocks many doors, grab hold of it. This exercise, as with all of them, is a step on the path to finding Your Voice, your Soul's Desire. It takes time and practice; you're doing it, don't stop now.

Acknowledge.

What does it mean to acknowledge something?

> *Definition: Acknowledge. To admit to be real or true; recognize the existence, truth, or fact of.*

When we acknowledge where we are in our life, and honestly look at it, we can begin to change the outcome or situation. You, my friend are changing. Keep at it, so

"Today you are you! That is truer than true! There is no one alive who is you-er than you!" Dr. Seuss

CHAPTER 5

Choosing Acceptance in Order to Grow

Are you someone who recognizes acceptance? Is acceptance even on your radar? How does acceptance play a role in finding your deepest desire? How does this calm inner voice lead you to everything you desire? As you step up and find your real worth, see yourself more clearly, and begin to lean into your vulnerability, acceptance becomes as simple as taking off a wet raincoat after an unexpected downpour.

Let's face the biggest troublemaker I know: perfection. Just so we're clear, there is no such thing as perfect. Although, how often are you bombarded with magazine covers with beautiful looking women who have perfectly airbrushed faces and breasts, or families who wear perfectly matched clothing, drive shiny, dustless cars, and live in impeccably clean houses with well-manicured yards? Here in San Francisco, and while I lived in Los Angeles, I faced perfection like this every day. Perfection reveals itself in a multitude of ways, and I either judge it, I'm ignorant or I accept it. I have a choice; so do you.

After getting honest with ourselves and truly seeing where we're at in any given situation, we need to accept and move on in our life.

Moving ahead is not always an easy feat. It's easier to gloss over a paycheck that doesn't meet your expenses and continue to pay for lattes on a credit card. It can be downright humiliating to face the facts of your life and even your financial status, especially when you've been sold the dream of "Go to college, get your Masters. Afterward, you'll be employable and earn lots of money and be successful." Meanwhile, your pile of daily living expenses and bills from doctors and your old student loans continue to haunt you.

My client Erica finished her university tour, got the "Job," and worked solidly, living paycheck to paycheck in a city that was voted to be one of the most expensive places to live in the States. Erica had moved there after reading a story in a magazine. It stated that this city was full of culture and had a lively nightlife, both of which she dreamed of enjoying once she got out of her small town of Grass Valley. She worked hard and learned to play hard with her colleagues, buying rounds of drinks, saying yes to happy hours, and enjoying Sunday brunches with her new girlfriends.

The weekly expenses began to escalate, and while keeping up with her colleagues was starting to cripple her financially, she still kept up with them. When a new credit card came in the mail, she thought, "Well that's perfect timing,

I can pay my expenses with this new card, there is no interest until next year…"

Two years into her excursion, she woke up to her electricity being turned off and nothing in her refrigerator to eat. She was penniless. She had ignored the pile of bills that were unopened on her vanity, the overdraft charges from her bank now left her without a functioning bank account, and her once-dreamed-about extraordinary life had fallen apart. She couldn't understand why. She had done everything right. But had she? *No.*

She neglected to accept her situation, which had layers to review. She neglected the high student loan and the job she had accepted, which paid less than her living expenses. She ignored her Inner Voice, that questioned why she bought a latte every day, instead of buying bulk coffee and making it at home. She ignored the mere fact that she would be downright broke if she continued to live in this city, in this fantasy. Accepting the truth never entered her mind, she was too busy trying to arrange the life she couldn't afford. Eventually, she landed back on her parent's couch, with nothing but a suitcase. She faced bankruptcy. Defeated by her lack of honesty, and discipline, she finally accepted her financial situation, asked for help, and began working with a financial debt program. She slowly put her life together in a new way, one in which was better than she had planned. Upon moving home, she reunited with her first love.

Accepting our place in life is not easy. However, without being honest, without finding acceptance, we only prolong our yearning to be in our Soul's Desire.

When you finally become willing to look within to overcome any lies that you've been living with, you will see the truth that's in front of you. You can't change without first recognizing the debt, the negative bank account, the marriage that's been long over, the weight around your middle, the empty house, or the lack of meaning in your life. You must see it all, stare at it and tell it, tell it all, that you're done with it.

Once you're willing to do this, you begin to open your heart and go inside with your Soul leading you, trusting that you can overcome what lies ahead of you. It's then that the rusted lock on the shackled door of Acceptance can be opened.

Accepting doesn't mean we like it; hell, accepting doesn't even mean you have to agree with it, but accepting is a necessary tenet to changing. Acceptance is merely a neutral agreement with reality. You don't have to pretend, fight it, make up outlandish stories, resist, or swear it off. You can say, "Okay, this is my life, where I'm at... [insert whatever the situation may be]" (my daughter failed, I lost my job, my car was stolen, my mother has been diagnosed with cancer) and move on to the next necessary indicated step. There will always be essential action steps to take with acceptance. You must take them to move your life forward.

Definition: Compassion. Sympathetic pity and concern for the sufferings or misfortunes of others.

Even compassion can be a necessary action step in growing closer to your true self, remember this when you do not understand why you need to accept something. These actions propel us forward.

The Obstacles: We resist.

Every day, we hear a small voice within us. This voice shares every second of every moment—how we are to live, how to earn money, how to live properly— leaving us with hundreds of expectations for every waking thought. Here is the struggle: realizing which voice to listen to, the one who haunts, ignores, judges every move or the Voice who implies a safer route? Accepting the truth is usually not our first choice, but to be Connected and live within our Soul's Desire, we must listen, *carefully*.

Somewhere along the path, you may have realized that you were living a lie, but you ignored it and pushed it aside where you thought you'd never find it. You learn how to do this from those around you. As children, we watch how our parents react to others and to each other. We intuitively begin to depict what is true and what is false from monitoring behaviors and actions and reactions. Our brains are hardwired to movement, and even the most subtle movement reveals deceit.

As a child, you learned and were expected to understand that not everything needs to be discussed or talked about —that not every family is perfect, or that the families imperfections are to be addressed with anyone. You learned traits of dishonesty from everyone around you, and it became difficult to differentiate what is true and what is false in the world unless you're tuned in and listened to your inner voice. You've resisted seeing what is wrong when being beaten by a loved one or when having an affair with a married man. You've ignored any neglect and replaced it with self-sufficiency. You're good at that, and self-reliance has brought you far in your life. (Hallelujah!)

You've chosen to see the world painted a slightly different shade to fit in without being noticed. You've done this and you're now not living up to your inner desires. You know deep within something isn't quite right—your Soul's call is getting louder.

As you walk along your life path, perhaps you've chosen to stay stuck in old patterns and habits from childhood. Keeping the lies alive, ignoring the truth.

"If I put on this disguise, I'll become someone else."

"No one will see me shoplift this jewelry..."

"I'll order the french fries and then run to the bathroom and get rid of them, I can't gain any weight, my husband will get wandering eyes..."

Well, as adults we know that it's not that easy. These habits are engrained within us, deep grooves. No amount of pushing things under the rug, numbing, avoiding, lying, denying, or arguing with reality will change what we can't accept. Only accepting it will. This is why the tenet, or act, of acceptance is so powerful.

The minute you accept what is, you have the power to change *it*... but days, months, years, even decades can pass you by as you dance around what it is that needs to be accepted. Afraid that if you accept, it will mean being stuck with it forever, or that it will bring about change in your life. Afraid to see a reality you don't want—even if it's there—like the a kid in her disguise who thinks she's invisible and will never get caught stealing, yet lands in jail at some point!

Navigating acceptance means stepping into adulthood, being responsible, getting still, taking a deep breath, opening your heart and asking for the courage to face what you have not wanted to face. Navigating acceptance can be similar to saying, "Okay, I've got this, now let's move on."

The Truth: Accepting may be easier than you think.

One common way of accepting is plainly saying, "Okay, I agree that this is real." We often put up such *resistance* — we go to such extreme lengths to deny something — that when we actually accept, it's much less difficult than we think. Your mind can spin extraordinary stories and create life-threatening monsters. *Reality check!* Open your closet and see if that the spiky, grizzly toothed monster exists in real time! No, it doesn't. The stories you create steer you far from the truth, afraid of what you might discover, afraid of the unknown possibilities and what everything may mean. Only your Soul has the ability to overcome these often-outdated, shocking stories. It's your Soul that can face your fears and forge ahead. Facing facts, and moving on to what is, is where you want to live and be in your life.

Acceptance does not mean settling. Acceptance is a courageous act on any trailblazer's path. You have the power to accept anything in your life—you are capable.

EXERCISE: Get quiet.

Setting yourself free with rock number four.

Write down 3 mental trappings (anything that you don't like, beat yourself up over, lie about, etc.) that feel hard for you to accept, right now. Don't worry, I'm not going to ask you to dive in and change them. Just see if you can notice them. This may take some time. When you're done, you can throw out the paper. But start somewhere.

Here is a list of great examples that I have collected from women around the world:

"I find it hard to accept my husband's snoring every night." Gladys West

"I find it hard to accept that I never have enough money and can't go on vacation." Cindy James

"I find it hard to accept my generous hips." Nancy Freeman

"I find it hard to accept my daughter's health situation." Colleen Moore

"I find it hard to accept my boss on any given day!" Melissa Twinne

"I find it hard to accept that I am not in control of my life." Kim Grazer

"I find it hard to accept that the farm is not earning enough money." Liza Jones

"I find it hard to accept help. I feel horrible for burdening others with my problems, totally forgetting or ignoring how wonderful I feel when I get to help someone else." Ruth Rau

"I find it hard to accept owning my own business and the time it takes to build. I like things to happen NOW!" Selena Maestas

"I find it difficult to accept my son will one day not have his chubby, soft cheeks. I find it difficult to accept my kids will want to learn to drive. Oh and I find it difficult to accept I might need reading glasses!" Kathy Stowell

"I find it difficult to accept that technology will 're-place' connection with nature." Lindsay Pera

"I find it difficult to accept a world without physical books (I do hope we will never get there), a world where people are communicating more via their electronics than with one another (oh wait, that is already here) and that my sweet little boy will one day grow up, smell of B.O./dirty gym socks and not let me to smother him with kisses every single day." Jenn Aubert

If you had a difficult time coming up with your list (or not), I want you to give yourself a big pat on the back. I know it's not easy taking a thought out of your head and placing it on paper, but it's worth it.

Practice.

Everyday for the next two weeks write out any trappings then challenge yourself, see if you can start accepting one thing from your list per day. Do not skip this for 14 days. Notice if any resistance comes up with any particular obstacle. Perhaps it's that your kid won't eat dinner. Maybe it's that your weekend wine drinking has turned into a nightly habit, and you want it to stop but are afraid of not being able to or what that might mean. If and when there is resistance, say this statement:

"I accept this today—only today, and right now."

Start with acceptance; remember, acceptance does not mean you have to agree with the challenge/obstacle (your child's nightly dinner protests) or even like it. It simply means that you're seeing it, and acknowledging that moment's reality, you're empowering yourself with deep compassion. You are doing it, allowing. Grace Happens, watch for her. Accept just for today.

"You gain strength, courage and confidence by every experience in which you really stop to look fear in the face... You must do the thing you think you cannot do." Eleanor Roosevelt

CHAPTER 6
Cultivating Inner Strength

Strength comes from being disciplined. If you use a muscle, again and again, it inevitably gets stronger, right? If you participate in a meditation every morning and night, your mental agility becomes durable and flexible, your mind can find the calm wave in an ocean storm more quickly, and resilience builds as if it's effortless. You can become brilliant at just about anything you want, given the time, commitment, and practice. Yes, practice!

Too often, though, you tell yourself you don't have the time. You listen to another voice—a sneaky, often deceitful voice—whispering in the background of your daily life. You also listen to ideas that are carried around from the distant past or a near past moment, that are no longer yours or serve you. Perhaps you've also latched on to ideas of being weak, lacking discipline, you just don't have it in you. You think you don't have the talent to make it happen —to get back up and fight for what you think is right.

None of this is true or correct.

If you set your mind on something you desire, truly desire, and you don't sabotage it with fabricated stories, absurd excuses, and lack of discipline—you'd get what you want. And usually in a shorter amount of time than expected.

Cultivating inner strength is like this, too. As with any practice, if you show up—even just a little every day—you arrive at a new place, with a new skill, a stronger body, mind, and firmer determination. With inner strength, and dedication you learn to listen to your inner wisdom, your Soul's Desire. You hone in on how to separate the voices in your head from what you actually want and need. The old stories and excuses, no longer take away from your Soul's purpose and desire, they begin to fade and fall from you. Face your fears. Remind yourself that you can do hard things, again and again, until you reach a place of self-trust and inner fortitude. You'll begin to trust and rely on your inner voice—the Connection which leads you to your desire.

I want you to render yourself free from that debating society, that small voice which sends you on errands and coffee runs when it's not necessary. It holds you hostage in bad situations, it tells you that next time will be different, or that one more refill on the popcorn is okay when you're at the movies with the family—for heaven's sake, *it's the holidays!* But no, it's not okay.

Listen, I know these voices very well. Everyone has them. They've made me question everything. They've been caught telling me lies which were both good and bad. You know what I'm talking about, don't you? I also call those voices the nagging sisters. Differentiating these voices from our Soul's Desire takes time and effort in learning and familiarizing yourself with it. You might often believe this voice is leading you down the right path, but then you find yourself miles away from where you want to be. Listen carefully to the whisper.

I want you to fire your nagging sisters; quiet them down, step into your Soul's whisper, and get closer to your desire. I wrote a letter to my nags (who have names). It helped me clear away fear that lingered in my life. Here is an abbreviated letter that I wrote many years ago:

Dear Sisters,

Yes, that's right, you two! Are you paying attention to me? I want you to know that I have absolutely appreciated each and every time you snuck me into some crazy situation, where I had to force myself to make decisions that perhaps were not always the best for me. Remember that time you told me to get in the car with that dodgy old man and drive to Santa Cruz. I became so ill from his cologne. I couldn't move (literally)... that was a nightmare.

You, you whisper at night when I lie awake next to my husband who breathes heavily, and you tell me to run. You have told me to run in every relationship I've ever had. You have wanted me to be alone, without love for my entire life. I have suffered. I have run a couple of times, losing love.

Do you remember when you started telling me stories about Dan? You said he was sleeping with someone else, that he didn't deserve me. You got me to drive by his house at wee hours of the night and stalk him. I mean, who even does that? Yes, you got me to do that! I became a "stalker." He ended up breaking things off with me because I had become obsessed. I had never been like that before. You managed to break up the wildest sex I'd ever had in my life!

Yes, you two are always there, plotting in the background, exploiting my weaknesses. You're always whispering and giggling. Yes, I do listen and learn from my mistakes, but honestly, I want you to take the back seat and let me lead the way. I have appreciated all the care and thoroughness. You amaze me, but at this point, I honestly believe that I can walk boldly alone and make decisions based on what I can hear outside of my head, what I can see, and touch in real life. I need to listen to my heart now, not you.

I want to thank you so much for everything and for always being there, for trying to protect me and guide me. It seems that I have been forced to grow, and at this point, I wish to grow alone.

With love and care,

Lane

The first time going through this exercise, I was embarrassed and ashamed. I could not believe that I had allowed myself to be in so many unsettling situations. As a result of writing it out and getting the shame of being a stalker on paper, I began to be free from those voices. This exercise made room for clarity and safety.

I want you to take out a pen and paper and draft a formal letter to the voices in your head. If you have an issue with the term "voices in your head," then think nagging sisters, or think of the troublesome voice that causes problems! Explain that you are firing them; they are no longer needed. As you write this letter, make sure to be sincere and share stories—use specific examples as I did in mine (Dan and the drive to Santa Cruz)—on how they may have helped you in hard times, and how they have perhaps gotten you through your life in challenging situations up to this point.

Express your gratitude to them, for without the nagging sisters, your life would be very, very different! After you have written this letter, I want you to read it out loud to yourself in the mirror. I know this sounds quacky, but it's proven to work. So just go for it! Close the door and read it out loud. You might want to do this a couple of times. Don't put the letter in a drawer and say you'll do it tomorrow, or on the weekend. After reading it, rip it into tiny pieces or burn it; say goodbye, for good!

Remember, your keywords here are sincerity and gratitude—always with an open, honest, and vulnerable heart.

The Obstacle: One word — Fear.

Are you familiar with this statement from Elizabeth Appell:

> *"And the day came when the risk to remain tight in a bud was more painful than the risk it took to blossom."*

Well, it couldn't be more apropos here. The only thing stopping you from meeting your inner strength and discovering all the places it can take you, is you.

The Truth: We are powerful beyond measure.

Marianne Williamson said it best in her book, *A Return to Love*:

Our deepest fear is not that we are inadequate. Our deepest fear is that we are powerful beyond measure. It is our light, not our darkness that most frightens us. We ask ourselves, "Who am I to be brilliant, gorgeous, talented, fabulous?" Actually, who are you not to be?

You are a child of God. Your playing small does not serve the world. There is nothing enlightened about shrinking so that other people won't feel insecure around you. We're all meant to shine. We were born to make manifest the glory of God that is within us. It's not just in some of us; it's in everyone. And as we let our own light shine, we unconsciously give other people permission to do the same. As we are liberated from our own fear, our presence automatically liberates others.

There had been so many times in my past when I'd walk into a room, and shrink just to fit in with the size of the room. It never felt right. Does that make sense to you? Yes, me. I shrunk in size, dimmed my light, turned down my enthusiasm, and got quiet, shut myself up to fit in and not create too much attention. I've always noticed when eyes would turn to me, gaze and look away, not inviting me into their conversation or even having the courtesy of saying hello. Awkward.

My life has been full of these moments, like the first time I walked into a business meeting full of women, with my son crying and hanging on me. No one said a word. I let the silence settle over everyone for a few minutes, I calmed my son and then said hello to the entire room in a steady, cheerful voice. All eyes wandered back to me, mouths began to curl with smiles, and they all started to say hello. The opportunity was there to stay small and have my son see others ignore us rudely, but I wouldn't have it. I feel obligated to share and demonstrate to my son how to rise to the occasion—approach a room that feels awkward and make it comfortable. Finding my inner strength and not listening to the negative voices, the nagging sisters, that initially said, "Don't worry, you won't get noticed, your son is being annoying and you have nothing to bring to this conversation."

In reality, I had a lot to bring to their attention, and I ended up helping many of the women in the room that night. Staying small, disconnected, and ignoring your Soul's Desire defeats the purpose of why you are here. You and I are here to help others. For me that night, it was about saying hello, starting the conversation, and creating a bigger community of women. Not listening to those voices is instrumental in being Connected and landing in Grace.

EXERCISE: Get quiet.

Flexing your inner voice with rock number five.

For 14 days, stop asking other people's opinions. Don't run a scenario by your husband, friend, colleagues, no, don't do it, don't ask for opinions. Keep your own counsel. Don't ask a girlfriend if your jeans look okay. Don't pretend to know *everything,* simply be sure in your thinking—it's okay. Practice getting still from Chapter 2 and begin to recognize your own inner voice. Then see what this voice is telling you.

Over this two week period, you will get to know the

sound, tone, and attitude of this inner voice—whether it be strict, funny, sarcastic, or even moody. You'll also find out what it wants and doesn't want, and what it thinks. Pay attention to where it resides, is it your heart, your gut, or a soft place right between your ears. Sometimes it speaks tenderly: a quick "no" before reaching for a second donut might be what has been ignored for years, and now the reason for being thirty pounds overweight? Or it's a gut feeling about a new coworker who doesn't have your back and is looking to move into your position. Whatever it is, start to notice it. Take notes to remember over this two-week period.

Practice:

After doing the 14-day exercise above, write down 3 *instructions* this inner voice has given you. Connect them with what actually happened in your day-to-day life. What are the differences, if any, on how you moved from week to week, keeping in mind the three instructions that you heard? Write down how this inner voice is guiding you to be your best self. Start to recognize this inner voice. *It's within you for a reason.* It wants you to live your best life—a life that you are meant to live. You have been created with a Divine Purpose. It's time to listen and start creating with it.

There are many times throughout the day where these thoughts, ideas, and creative sparks are left unspoken, you skip over them, sometimes by accident, but usually not. What I see and experience is a slow build of discontent, and with that, trouble builds. Grief centers on things that are unsaid—what are you holding on to that you haven't said? **Write down** what you have not said, shared, or what you've held back in your life, place these ideas gently in your notebook. Healing can happen more quickly when we look at everything and live by our unique voice. No one else's opinion matters. Reveal yourself more and more, you've got this.

Learning more about yourself can be frightening, but what do you have to lose? You've come this far, don't ignore what you bring to the world.

Make sure to check in with yourself and meditate with your free meditation.

> "Success is not final, failure is not fatal, it is the courage to continue that counts." Winston Churchill

CHAPTER 7

Finding and Implementing Your Worth

One of the many side effects of finding your voice and living within your Soul's Desire is learning your worth. You are incredibly valuable; you know this deep down inside, so listen.

At Work.

How valuable are you? When you begin to evaluate your worth in your working environment, one of the greatest assets or tools that you have in relation to the company is finding the power to speak up about what matters to you. And, having the capacity to share it in conversations. Your unique perspective can change everything—in your relationship, in your office, in your company, or even with a stranger on the street who could become your next business partner or venture.

There can also be moments when you have the ability to share your desire with your company, and it turns out to be a minority opinion. Have you ever had the opportunity to listen to someone who is passionately against the norm? When they are bold enough to speak up and share their point of view strongly enough, others may listen and change their own point of view. This turns the discussion in an entirely different direction and is a result of being *connected.*

My client, Kali, who happens to be African-American, found this exact moment when she shared her opinion in a board meeting and changed the entire vote. I mention that she is African-American only for reference, as the topic that was being discussed was racial. Her unique perspective changed the viewpoint of the entire room of white male colleagues. This was an amazing, triumphant moment for Kali, who often was overlooked in many conversations. The simplest way to find your worth is by tuning in and listening to this voice we are working on finding. Listen with open ears. Listen without any judgment.

How do you find your worth at work?

I do this by asking myself to be present. It's that simple. I say something like this: "Let me just show up in this conversation and be entirely present. Let me listen to what they have to say." If I can do that, then I can learn how to best serve the situation, business, or company. I have also learned there are times when not saying anything is the next indicated choice and the best way to assist the organization. Often when we don't say anything, we are speaking loud and clear to our colleagues, employers, or employees. Saying *nothing* is sometimes just as loud as saying *something.*

Are you clear on what you contribute to your organization? Most women show up at a job and work aimlessly, on autopilot, completing a task list the length of a desk. Are you genuinely caring about everything that you do for the company, or are you merely looking to collect a paycheck? I want you to become clear about what it is that you contribute to the company—what is your expertise, your specialty? Do you know? Or have you forgotten because you've been given a huge to-do list?

For a moment, examine what you excel in within the enterprise. *Write it down now*. I want you to take note of the nagging sisters that may pop up in your mind; they will not be helpful in this evaluation. Try not to compare yourself to anyone. When evaluating your worth in your workplace, it's important to ask yourself what your greatest strengths are, and then sincerely recognize them. What is it that you bring to the table that no one else does? Having clarity—knowing your worth— will change the dynamics and relationship that you have with your company, your business. You matter.

Finding your worth with money.

Let me ask you this: are you being compensated financially for your worth (not necessarily what you do, but what you're worth)? Have you clearly defined what you do, and what you bring to the company, job, family, to the world? Are you being recognized for your contributions to a greater whole or purpose? Everyone is important in a company; everyone holds value. When it comes to your Soul's Calling and Divine Purpose, we have to be in alignment with money. Are you asking what does that mean? I'll say it again—it's simple. *You matter*. What you contribute is valuable, and although women still get paid less than men, you have to recognize your importance, and the value you bring. Have you done that? What are you worth? **Write it down**. Can you assign a numerical value to your efforts? Is it $15 an hour, $300 an hour, or $500,000 a year? Write down that number and look at it. Can you own that number?

Without owning that number, and without knowing it within your Soul's Desire, you won't reach it, attain it, or even be given the opportunity to create that wealth.

Is it time for you to get a raise? I'm going to guess and say it is—*right?* You've been working hard, you've given your all, you've given more. It's time. Let's get a raise, let's ask for what you're worth, your valuable. In your notebook, write down what you've done, what you've created, and how you've contributed to your company, your family, even the world as a whole. How are you serving the world? Don't fret about what you have partially done or have not done, yet.

Next, what would you like to earn? What does it cost for you to live and thrive in your life? Not scraping by every month and living paycheck to paycheck—what does it honestly cost for you to enjoy your life? I'm talking go to movies, eat out, eat organic, take classes, send your kid to particular activities, go on extended holidays, fly to the other side of the world in business class? Take time to consider this, and be *honest*. When it comes to money matters, we must be concise. Money likes vision and speed. Write down an *exact* number and **own** it. If you can't own the number, it's not going to happen. How do you own the number? Good question. See it in your bank account. Envision yourself depositing money. Meditate on your money. When you have done this, you can begin to work on formulating a conversation that you will bring to your boss or manager about what you're worth and what you have thus far executed in your position. If you own your company and are ready to level up, then owning that number you wrote down is a *must.* Just as importantly, it's *your* company! It's your wealth; you deserve it!

One of the many ways I have my clients begin to own their worth financially is by writing the number down several times a day; visualize it. Then I suggest they say it out loud to themselves in the first person, the second person, and then as a narrative person. You can also get creative with these sentences.

For example: I, (your name), am worth $300,000. She is worth $300,000. That woman, (your name), is worth $300,000.

I know I am worth $75,000. She is worth $75,000. That woman is worth $75,000.

Our brain—remember the prefrontal cortex, the executive area, decision maker—*makes this happen*. Part of our brain begins to take action when we talk to ourselves this way. My client Sandy used this exact method to level up when she was consulting with an individual company. Here are the sentences she came up with:

"Sandy, you've got this, it's only $200,000 more a year."

"Sandy, $200,000 this year is the right amount to enjoy and share."

"Sandy, this year another $200,000 will happily afford an additional holiday and Beth's school tuition. I'm loving the ability to choose this for my daughter"

Notice the word happily in that last sentence. Emotion is

so important when we begin to call *into* our worth. How will that $200,000 feel? And how will it feel to pay for holidays and tuition? When you sink into an emotion and take note of how you feel, I want you to commit to that emotion, stay with it, be unattached to an outcome after you have made the statement and stay in the emotional frequency. Each emotion carries a vibration, that vibration will either attract or repel what it is that you want. Your high vibrations can change everything, I promise.

She's also said something like this every once in a while: "I'm going to earn an extra $200,000 this year, *effortlessly.*"

"She is easily receiving $200,000 this year—so simple!"

Once you begin doing this, **don't stop**. When you stop, your desire putters out. Seriously, don't stop. Just for extra credit, write it down in your journal every day. As you become comfortable with these statements, your ideas on what you contribute to the world and your perception of your **value** will change. Your Soul's Desire will begin to surface, and your life will shift gears. Your financial motor will rev up and begin to produce results. Keep the motor running—maintain that engine. Stay emotionally tuned into those feelings, and your financial worth will grow.

I just mentioned that you can't stop. As soon as you become comfortable with the amount and know your worth without a doubt, ask your company for a raise. If you are working at a company, make sure to write down what you have been doing in the company, what you are *sincerely* worth, and the number that you are asking. **Do not hesitate**. Your confidence will get you your raise if you are clear minded, direct, and state your Soul's Desire. Do not go into your boss's office and *wing it* — please do not overlook this part of the process. (Yes, this is a warning.)

Before you go barging into your manager or boss's office, make sure to ask if they would take a moment with you to discuss your job. Here's one of those passing moments of intimidation—where the *Nagging Sisters* can, and are likely to, chime in and share their voices. However, if you have invested your time wisely and have done the work, then you know how valuable you are! You *must* (I don't like to use the word must a lot, but in this case, it is a must) write it down, and rehearse speaking to your boss, HR person, whoever is in charge. Practice asking and sharing about your worth and value. Only then, you are ready to walk in and own the conversation. (Find your voice and ask Grace to help you at that moment, you can do it!) Before meeting with your boss or supervisor, make sure that you take a private moment and review—connect with yourself, read aloud what you have written down in your notebook, what you have contributed, what you are worth, what you are asking for, and why it's important. Truly *feel* the raise; feel good, excited, happy, and worthy. Keep your emotional state high.

It is essential that you step in and own your worth in this conversation. The more conviction you have, the more likely you'll be heard, noticed, and given what you are asking—if the company has the resources. The next action to take is to invite someone to listen to your request (do a test run). Have this person give you feedback or fire back objections so you will have fast answers if asked. After this step has been done, you are ready! Take action and ask for what you are worth.

Keep me posted—check in on my page and let me know!

Your worth in relationships.

Your sense of self-worth reveals itself in this arena every day. Do you feel like you're picking up the slack in your relationships? Do you ever feel like the doormat? Or that you do more than your share of *everything*? Do you feel like you're not getting back what you give? Or that you lack boundaries, out of fear of what the other person will say/do/think? Your relationships are shaped by an inner dialogue that is based on your very own self-worth. Big statement, right? Well, let's think about this. Take a moment and remember what it was like in your house as you were growing up. Were you an only child, smothered with love? Were you the middle child of three and ignored, or the youngest and luckiest because your mom had complications? Whatever the case, this was the beginning of your self-worth.

When we are raised in a house with a mother who is there, attentive, and responsive to our needs, we lean into more confidence. We don't seek the same attention another person would who was raised by someone who had little parenting or minimal attachment. Your self-worth started years ago; it began before you even had a chance. I see this every day with my clients. Your inner self-worth is foundational to being a strong, vibrant, healthy woman in today's world.

I want you to *know* that you don't have to pick up the slack any longer. You don't have to be the one always doing everything. It's not your job to be the *doer*. Your job is to be in your work and to be equal in relationships—this includes your marriage and any other relationship. You are not lower and not above, but equal in relationships with everyone.

Relationships are built on mutual trust and mutual respect. That is a great measurement to strive for. We're all equal, and once you wrap your head around that thought, your world will change. Think about that in your personal relationships—girlfriends hanging around sharing, no gossiping, no ducking out of conversations that are difficult. Even at your office you are equal. Yes, you can have a boss and colleagues who are higher in the chain of command, perhaps they are further along in their skill set, but as far as importance and what matters—all people are equal. Perhaps your boss does know more than you, has more experience, but when you shift to bigger thinking with your Soul's Desire, it is your unique perspective and experience that makes the task/job completed by you special.

The job that gets executed by you is special. Your Soul's Purpose and Desire is unique, and no one else is capable of executing it like you. Let me restate that, only your unique perspective can create a story and tell it from your point of view. No one else is able to share exactly like you. If you're a painter, no one else holds the brush as you do, or mixes paints as you do, or applies the paint on the canvas as you do. What you do is special. The way that you move on the street, in a classroom, in an office, in a boardroom, is unique to you. It's your energy and fills the space as no one else can. You are unique. No one else can be compared to you for what you bring to the world. Your Soul's Desire can only be brought by you.

Your writing, your voice, your opinions matter. No one has your exact perspective or thumbprint.

In your marriage, your partner or husband is not above

you. He/she is not one to dictate how you spend money, how to cook a dinner, or even to put gasoline in the car. And, yes, I have heard all of these as examples from my clients who have disconnected from their partner and their own Soul's purpose. *Connection!* Your partner is equal to you—not above or below you. Relationships built from honesty generate mutual respect, trust, and admiration.

Stacey came to a session recently with a belittling story about her and her husband. It shocked me a little to hear this, but I knew it was true from how she spoke about the incident.

"Lane, he has no idea how I feel. He won't listen to me, and last night he attacked me."

My first questions were if her daughter was in the house when this happened, and if she saw the altercation.

"No, she was with my mother for the weekend. Since she was away, I thought it was the perfect time for us to talk about the house and how our relationship felt to me. Boy was that the wrong thing to do. He became defensive immediately, yelled that he didn't want to talk about it, and walked away. I didn't want him to walk away, so I naturally raised my voice and said, 'We need to deal with this; I can't live like this anymore.' Lane, this is the moment I will never forget. He turned with a look in his eyes I'd never seen and immediately approached me, then raised his hand and hit me. I felt broken and powerless; I didn't know what to do. I grabbed the side table lamp and threw it at him. He blocked it, then grabbed me and shook me. Staring into my eyes, he said, 'If you don't like it here, you can leave!'."

Stacey was crying as she retold her story. She was devastated, as any woman would be at that moment. We take vows with our partner for better or worse, and we never anticipate or expect to be touched in a way that is humiliating and fills us with fear.

"What do I do?" She asked.

I stayed with her for a minute and allowed her years of tears to seep from her eyes; she was tired and lost. I held the space for her to be.

"Stacey, do you want to leave? This is your first option, or do you want to stay? He has made it clear to you that you have a choice—*you* have to decide."

"After he walked out, I ran out of the house and took a long walk. I was gone for most of the day. I went back to the house around 5:00, and he was sitting on the couch. His eyes were bloodshot, and he looked as if he'd aged ten years; it was so sad to me. I walked in, and he started crying to me about how sorry he was and that he didn't mean to hit me. Lane, I didn't know what to do. I sat there with him and remembered all the work that you and I have done over the past six months. I paused from saying it was okay—it wasn't okay! I broke from yelling at him more; I *paused* from getting up and packing my bags.

Instead, I listened. Lane, it worked. I listened to my Soul's Calling, my *deepest desire*. Connection. Then I said, 'Stu, we need help, you need help, and if we want to remain married and have a family together, we have to participate in this marriage. You are not the boss of me; I am not the boss of you. We can both call it quits right now, but I can share that this-this that happened today—will be the last time it ever happens. I will never have you touch me again as you did. You have no right to lay a finger on me as you did and I will not hold it against you, I will never mention it again, but you have to get help. We have to find help.'."

I'd love to share that the story has a happily-ever-after ending, where Stacey and Stu are romantically swept off in their lives, but the happily ever ending is entirely different. Stacey ended up leaving her marriage. Stu thought he wanted help, he said he wanted help, but acted out again on Stacey several weeks later, before they had a chance to take their relationship to the next place. Stacey found the courage to leave her marriage. She knew deep within herself it wasn't working. Stu's action made her feel inferior, belittled, unloved, neglected, and definitely not an equal partner. Stacey drew her line in the sand, she was *done* living in fear. She wouldn't have it. She found her deepest desire; her Soul's Calling. We worked on an exit plan that would not interrupt her daughter's life, and she left, taking her daughter and moving in with her sister. Not the scenario she wanted at 38, but a scenario that was safe—where she could rebuild herself and not have her daughter grow up to be a victim.

"I had to leave. I can't have my daughter see the bruises on my arm, or grow up with a mother who neglects the truth. I don't want my daughter to be like me and end up in an abusive relationship. My mother was married to my dad for 25 years and I saw what he did to her. I loved my dad, and at the time I didn't understand why he would hit my mom, but now 35 years later it makes sense to me. I love Stu, but I can't allow abuse—any kind of it—on me or my daughter."

Stu was never physically abusive with their daughter, but

he raged in the evenings, placing a thread of fear within their daughter. Now, Stacey is learning how to maintain her autonomy and be in the world in a new way as a bold, independent woman and mom. She connected with her deepest desire and learn how to walk on her own, with her own self-worth.

For a moment I want to circle back to honesty because —like I talked about in Chapter 4: "Getting Honest"—you have to take a look at how you behave. Are you overlooking or forgiving someone's bad behavior out of your own fear of rejection or missing something you think should or shouldn't happen? Or in this case with Stacey, fear of losing a marriage.

> *"My heart leads, as my mind betrays me. I cry alone and no one can see me. I wake with pain, and pulled to the day with fear. Fear runs my life as I live alone but not. People surround me, constantly, noise interferes, and I wait until one day, I can walk alone with a smile and no more tears."* Unknown 2001

Can you see how connecting with your Soul's Calling is multi-dimensional, and how you *might consider* paying attention to *everything*?

It's imperative that you understand this part of the journey—stating your worth and equality to others. We are all walking around in the world, important and busy. We are all born the same way. We start in utero and come out; we all pass at some point as well, back to ashes and *Mother Earth*. We all have within us something that is buried deeply, waiting to be revealed and shared with the world. It's often deeply concealed, or never heard or revealed out of fear, out of this illusion of not being good enough, or it not making sense. You are worth more than you know, keep listening.

You may have days where you might be thinking, *why am I not famous, why haven't I risen in the ranks, I've done my part, I've stepped up as much as I can.*

Sorry, I'm going to say you haven't. I'm going to go out on a limb here and talk about some people on this planet who are extraordinary—in the sense that they ascended to the occasion. Not because of anything in particular, but because they made an agreement with their inner desire —their Soul's Purpose—perhaps even by mistake. Some people call this luck.

I don't believe Mark Zuckerberg was trying to do anything but be himself when he started sharing the first Facebook campus groups. I don't believe that Edison was trying to be magnificent; no, he was simply *obsessed* with doing what he knew how to do—create. Oprah followed her calling against all odds. We are all coming in and out of this world the same way, and it's our **job** to find our purpose, Deep Desire, our voice, and spread what we're doing *equally*. No one is above us, and no one is below us; we all have the same opportunities. It's when we link up with our Connection, raise up our vibration, and tap into emotion that our life changes and shifts dramatically. Gwen Stefani tore up her pants and jackets, shaved her head, said *no* to her mom, and sang her heart out. *She listened.* You, too, have the same opportunity to rise up; what are you doing about it today?

In Chapter 3, I talked about how listening to your inner voice and acting upon it builds and improves your communication, the way you move about in the world, and how you are seen and heard. I also shared how listening to that voice is like working out—the more you work out, the stronger you get, the leaner you become. The same principle applies here as well. The more you tune in, the easier it is to rise up and reveal your gift, your creativity, your answers. This is what the world needs: your vision, your inner creativity, your truth, your Connection, your Soul's Desire.

You can choose to have equality with your employers, friends, partners, family members, and your colleagues. You need to be shameless—no inner dialogue of disgust, fear, or shaming yourself. Living in equality is empowering. You are equal.

The Obstacle: Perfection.

You already know perfectionism is a huge weakness, and you also know it's an obstacle to many things, including happiness, peace, and owning who you are. You don't have to change yourself to be loved. You don't have to be someone else to get a raise or have the things you want. *You are already enough*. Step down from all the dysfunction in your life and connect with yourself. Any lingering belief of you not being enough, or that you are less than, bad, wrong, imperfect, or unworthy needs to go, needs to be removed. These obstacles stand in the way of what's true—you are worthy. Connect to your deep inner voice, and know that you are perfectly imperfect.

The Truth: We are all equal.

We humans have the tendency to compare and despair. We

put others on a pedestal or tell ourselves we are somehow better than the next—smarter, thinner, prettier. In the end, none of this really matters. We are who we are. They are who they are. No one is better—or worse. Perhaps richer or poorer but that is inconsequential, and those comparisons are generally only ever based on a snapshot in time that is no indication of what someone's life reveals in the long run. We are all worthy. We all deserve love; we all have potential. We all make mistakes.

None of us are perfect. We are equal.

Practice:

Every day for 30 days, give yourself *something* you want. Yes! I give you permission to do this. Many women can't or won't do this. If you are not ready to do this—and as surprising as it sounds right now, you'll see the challenge—it's hard to give to yourself. Spend the first five days noticing and allowing what you want, even if you don't give it to yourself. During these 30 days, give yourself small wants, small desires, they can and will grow over time, but let's begin small.

    Example:

    Day 1: I want to nap.

    Day 2: I want another cup of coffee.

    Day 3: I want that scarf.

    Day 4: I want to talk to Julie this weekend.

    Day 5: I want to feel excited about something again.

After the first five days, begin to practice giving to yourself, no matter what. If you don't know how, or you feel you can't do it immediately, that's okay. Just note it. And then notice what comes up for you—what thoughts or feelings do you notice around giving yourself what you want? Do you feel guilty? Silly? Do you think you will get "too used to this"? Lose your motivation in life? Write all this down. I want you to get in touch with the emotion of different desire. Different desires bring you different energy—and different vibrations. For example, my desire for another cup of coffee brings me a bit of giddiness because I'm being "sneaky." I know I shouldn't have a second cup because I'll be up at midnight. That feeling of giddiness is different than the vibrant, peaceful feeling you get after a nap—a delicious, nourishing nap... get it? I want you to pay attention to emotion, remember our emotional state changes everything!

EXERCISE: Get quiet.

Name three times when you have been in a situation where you felt "less than." What was going on around you? Who was there? What do you think contributed to this feeling? How do you wish it were different?

For example, you're dropping your kid off at school, and another mom shows up wearing gorgeous boots, a belt around a cashmere sweater, her hair done perfectly, and it's only 8:30 in the morning. You're still in sweatpants! You suddenly feel like a slob—yep, that's feeling "less than." *Just notice this.*

When you're through writing out your moments of feeling less than or not enough, take a long moment to reflect on these experiences. Chances are, these all offer insight into what you want more of for yourself. It's not about feeling envy of someone else's ability to look good, or feeling unworthy. If you want to dress well to drop your kid off at school, *do it.* What's stopping you? Likely the things that are stopping you *(I can't afford it, I don't have time to do my hair in the morning)* are all based on limiting beliefs you have about your own worth— you see how this is all tied together? It doesn't have to be! These limiting beliefs are what we need to rewire.

When you put your head on your pillow at night, it's just you, and you, alone on that pillow, unless of course you have someone snoring next to you. When you retire at night, fall asleep with a meditation to begin rewiring the deep grooves. You are worth everything your heart desires. You work hard for what you want, now believe in yourself and start taking action for those desires. You haven't been brought here to this time in your life on accident; there are no coincidences that you picked up this book. When clients reach me, they're ready. Just like you, you are ready to get to the next level and fulfill your purpose. I believe in you.

"Life is not easy for any of us. But what of that? We must have perseverance and above all confidence in ourselves. We must believe that we are gifted for something, and that this thing, at whatever cost, must be attained." Marie Curie

CHAPTER 8

Following Your Own Path in Confidence

If you're reading this book, you're seeking a path that everyone wants to be on, but can't find. Yet, here you are. You've made it this far and have been working patiently through the exercises—you're slowly waking up and beginning to hear your voice. You're becoming vulnerable with yourself; that's all that matters. You're telling the truth, accepting and moving forward—yes, you're finding a way to the path that is yours: your Divine Purpose, your Soul's Calling.

Walking your path takes **courage**. You will constantly step back in line and move forward with an open heart. It's an ongoing practice, for a good long time. You'll start to see the huge payoffs along the way, I promise.

Then one day you'll understand that being in *connection* is just like breathing. Soon, you'll wonder who that person was who used to hide, lie, and be motivated by fear. And, perhaps, wish you'd done this sooner.

The Obstacles: The Inside and the Outside.

Often, we are focused on the outside *stuff*, we lose total connection with ourselves and with what's going on inside. This disconnection leads to a whole host of issues—a breeding ground for lying, hiding, playing small, and shutting down. We follow others and then look for their approval. We fear failing, or have a fear of fear itself. Perhaps we turn in on ourselves, demanding perfection, or shaming ourselves for not being good enough. Ultimately losing in the game of life, we become resentful, unfulfilled, and so far from our Divine Purpose that we walk along dreading our lives—empty.

You're almost done with this guide, and if I only teach you one universal principle, I want it to be this: **You are enough on this journey.** Raise your vibration, and life will happily meet you.

The Truth: It's Our Job as Humans to BE.

Remember, we all have our *own* path. And it's our job to find it, get on it, and follow it. Our job here on earth as humans is not to robotically do what we think others— our parents, friends, boss, partners—want us to do. It's not too speak, behave, or be as we imagine others would want.

Or to spend our lives paralyzed in fear...

Our job here on earth is to be who we are, to operate from a place of truth to the person we are, and walk the path of our Soul's Desire. Each of us has a soul contract, don't waste it on living small, and being disconnected.

EXERCISE: Get quiet.

The sixth rock we move gets stuck again and again, let's reset it completely.

Write down three obvious, or not so obvious areas in your life where you feel you are not truly being whom you are meant to be on this planet. Are you walking a path someone else created for you, or is it a path you think others want you to be on with them?

Next to these three areas, write what you'd like to be doing instead... what would feel more aligned with who you are today? You do not need to take action at this point or even do anything—simply recognizing these areas and writing what you want instead will begin to wake up, and activate your RAS.

Practice:

This practice is ongoing... if you want to start moving toward living the life of you (and no one else), and experiencing more joy, more love, more peace, and more of who you are... go back to the above exercise and start building out action steps you can take—small ones at first—then build to bigger steps.

Breathe.

You're almost there.

> *"Faithless to be yourself in a world that is constantly trying to make you something else is the greatest accomplishment."* Ralph Waldo Emerson

CHAPTER 9

Finding Your True North: Years of Culmination

Your Soul's Calling is the happy place you feel comfortable in—it's the place that feels natural for you. It's like breathing.

In this book, I have outlined a few significant ways we resist or block our truth, our inner voice; not allowing ourselves to become who we are meant to be on this planet at this time.

Often when we are most uncomfortable, we should jump, and trust that we will land on our feet and become whom we are meant to be.

Take, for example, my client Jessica. She is a triathlete, a natural-born runner. All of her life she'd been running. She started in grade school, alongside her father, running on the weekends. She went to college on a scholarship for running long distance and got a business degree for "business" sake. Because she had to do something with her life, she opened up an accounting business for mid-sized companies, following in her accountant father's footsteps. When she found me, not only was she miserable, but she was twenty pounds overweight and had no idea why she was so sad every day. Together, we decided to dig into her history. Immediately we found gold!

Upon asking her a series of questions, Jessica revealed that she couldn't stand *numbers*, or the snobby business owners who were her clients. I also asked her the question that moved all my clients, *if she could do anything, right then and there, what it would be?* Immediately she replied: *RUN!* Her entire being lit up, she became radiant; life changing.

We ended that session with a simple suggestion that she go home, put on her running gear, and run. She did! The next day she called and told me that she hadn't felt that good in years. I could hear in her voice that we were on to something, that we needed to dig into her running. I worked with Jessica for six months uncovering her Soul's Purpose, although, in reality, she truly uncovered it in that first conversation. I knew that running would somehow be included with her *Soul's Calling, her True North*.

In those six months we rearranged her life, created a practice and action plan so that she could take her company to the next level both operationally and financially. Ultimately she hired a COO and took the back seat to her company, this action plan and practice moved her life in an entirely new direction. She is back on track with running —it's in her life practically every day. She stepped into her true self. Made a plan to enter competitive triathlons, lost twenty pounds, and is no longer perpetually sad. She found the courage to look under the sadness and dig into a simple question: *If you could do anything right now, what would it be?*

No one gets it right the first time, or even the second or third time, this practice stuff, takes work and time. We all go through the muck and grind of trying so hard, doing something that we *think* we should be doing, only to find ourselves feeling defeated, and unhappy. We get bruised on this journey of self-discovery and skin our knees too. Most people hide all their blemishes with a lot of makeup or Band-Aids. I want you to start sharing the muck, the real, and the pesky blemishes. Every time you fall down, tell someone, own your vulnerability, set the stage for change. Rip off those Band-Aids!

Change takes time. Time takes time. Period.

When I was four and three quarter years sober, 9-11 hit, and I seriously thought the end of the world was coming. My roommate frantically bombarded my room, blasting in at 6:45 a.m., turning Fox News on the television. The clip they kept repeating was that of the collapse of the Towers. I was mesmerized with the image, and my stomach turned and dropped. It was eerie, and left me feeling empty.

Hours later, my then, for lack of a better word, boyfriend, showed up and wanted to get a puppy. The streets of LA were empty. My head was quiet. We drove to the SPCA in silence, not knowing what to say or do. Arriving at the SPCA, and looking into the cages, I knew that I no longer could be in the U.S.—it was as if a light switch turned on in my head. I didn't say anything, but in my gut, I knew I had to leave. We walked the aisles of the shelter to find small and large lonely dogs all looking for homes, for people to love them and share a good life with them. I couldn't provide that and told him I wanted to leave. We drove back to my house only to find my roommate still in a panic from the morning event. It was a strange day. Fox News was again blasting through our apartment, and all I wanted to do was pack my bags. I didn't do anything. I watched and listened for my inner voice.

A couple of days later I ended up at the once highly-loved, new-age bookstore, The Bodhi Tree, in West Hollywood, browsing the many shelves of *self-help* books. I came across William James book, The Varieties of Religious Experience: A Study in Human Nature. I bought it and took it home. I read it, thirsty for more, I wanted answers. I tried to understand why we, the United States, were just attacked, and why no one was doing anything about it. What was happening? I read all day, all night, after reading that book, something shifted within me. I had a *new* calling. It was now my job to let go of the life I had created, and discover this force from within, and follow my Soul's Calling.

A month later, my roommate and I held our annual Thanksgiving dinner with twenty five or our close friends. I announced that I was leaving—packing and selling all my belongings to be of service to those in need on the other side of the world. My friend's mouths dropped with shock. I told them that I *had* to leave. I felt like I didn't have a choice. I knew my inner voice was calling me to help women in an unknown way. I decided to travel to the other side of the world and be of service to an institution assisting women to escape from prostitution. I also ended up helping children learn English at another institution.

I landed at some random hour after nineteen hours of air

travel and layovers. I awkwardly departed the plane and stepped onto the airport landing strip, the 103-degree heat washed over me like an old smelly electric blanket. I was beyond exhausted when I arrived, my senses screamed. The sour air was the perfect mix of jet pollution, cow dung, and trash; I was repulsed. I found my way to baggage and tried not to stare at the one-armed body who was dragging himself across the floor begging. I made it to the taxi stand without being bribed or hustled, and once safely inside the taxi I began to pray. I prayed that we would safely make it to the address I handed him on a piece of paper. We swerved through eight lanes of traffic; small cars, open air buses, large trucks, and thousands of two-wheeled vehicles moving about in all different directions. The smog was so thick I could barely see who was in front of us. Being in Bangkok for less than two hours brought me more than what I had bargained. Dirty children chased the taxi banging on the widows. Women with small children sat on the street begging for food. Everywhere I looked revealed poverty, scarcity, illness, and hopelessness.

What had I just done to my life? I left every known comfort and was now facing discomfort and fear in all areas of life.

Do you know what fear feels like? *Does it live in your stomach? Or does it show up in your head? Does it rob you from what could happen in your life or what you dream about every day?*

Being on the other side of the world, not knowing a language amongst eight million people, and not knowing how to connect with anyone, was a lonely place to be, but I survived. I fell into service which I came to love; I was so far from my big paychecks, fancy dinners and celebrities.

Living a life of service is not glamorous, but it is extremely fulfilling. Let me ask you again, yet in a slightly different way, what are you *not* doing that brings you joy?

EXERCISE: Get quiet.

Emotionally infuse the next two rocks we turn over on the path.

How many times do I have to ask... *If you could do anything right now, what would it be?* Write it down. Say it out loud, how does it feel? Pay attention to what you just said as you go about your day today, remember this is an emotional journey, infuse your answer with emotion. Journal on this answer.

Practice:

Use the exercises in this book as a guideline for where you still need work. Which exercises were most challenging for you? What questions so far have bothered you? Continue working on them daily.

Putting it All Together: The Action Plan for Finding Your Own Inner Voice:

1. Accept the past and where you're at right now.

2. Make a decision about (some) matters you want/or how you want to BE.

3. Write this all down on paper.

4. Write out the details of every action that need to happen.

5. Share with another person.

6. Be accountable to a group. (https://www.facebook.com/lanekennedy)

7. Keep taking action, no matter what, even when you want to stop.

8. Pay attention to how you feel: you must feel good, tingly, easy, rested, yummy, delightful, or even neutral when you are setting your life in motion. The way you feel will do all the attracting, so be aware and careful. Remember heart coherence.

As humans we have tendency to get stuck, don't worry, just keep coming back to the work of your life, you will get there. I promise.

> "When it's over, I want to say: all my life I was a bride married to amazement. I was the bridegroom, taking the world into my arms. When it is over, I don't want to wonder if I have made of my life something particular, and real. I don't want to find myself sighing and frightened, or full of argument. I don't want to end up simply having visited this world." Mary Oliver

CHAPTER 10
Revealing More & Closure

Pulling it all together is hard. Let's face it, most humans are settling for less than who they are meant to be, but you're not.

It's taken me four years to write this little book. Actually, it's been four long arduous years. I've tried to put this book to bed (*as in delete it, throw it out, and stop*) several times along the journey—not because I didn't know what I wanted to write or how to end it, but because it was too simple. For me what I share is simple, simplicity has always been a huge stumbling block.

I'm at the end now. Finally, I'm at the end of this book. I sit in Portland, Oregon, pondering how to close it up, how to wrap up my thoughts with a pretty bow. *Be done with it for God's sake!*

Every year for the past four years, I've come to Portland, Oregon in celebration with Chris Guilbeau, and a tribe of people for the World Domination Summit—a place where people come together to be inspired, to create, to release projects, and change the world.

This year I wasn't sure I was going to make it. Actually, I had planned on *not* making it, but then a good friend of mine said *let's go*. I had nothing to lose but everything to gain, as I had reached a new personal low in my life. The previous 12 months had been challenging, to say the least. I finished building a house that took three years of my life. I almost lost my marriage, and my health decided to take a turn for the worse and all areas of my life seemed like I was failing. I've never been a failure, it didn't feel good!

Making a decision to attend WDS wasn't about being inspired. I certainly didn't want to meet new people or see old friends. No, I wanted to attend WDS because I would be *alone*—away from my family, away from my work, and away from my house for a week. I knew during this time that nothing was going to happen. I had planned on *nothing* happening while I was away on this trip. I rented an Airbnb Loft in the Pearl District away from the WDS festivities, away from all of the hype. I needed space.

What I Realized:

I began writing this book as an experiment. Many of my clients repeatedly told me I should have a book or something to hand to someone. "Lane, write a book, please!" Four years ago, I was up for the challenge; I would create what they asked for, an easy to use resource. S*imple, I thought,* done!

I had a plan. I would write this guide; copying my techniques just as I was in the many sessions guiding women to their most critical tool in life, their Calling, that Inner Voice, the Soul's Connection. Four years into it I realized I was frustrated, feeling broken and I had lost touch with my own Soul's Calling. My plan, failed!

After landing in Portland, I sat in the loft the first night and cried. I didn't know what to do with myself. Exhausted, and alone, I went to bed. I woke up the next morning, did absolutely nothing, and stayed in my pajamas until 3 p.m., not feeling very motivated. I prayed. I tried to meditate, I tried to connect, but nothing happened. I sat alone in the loft, looking out the windows and watching people from above, wondering about their lives. I wondered what inspired them every day, and what gave them the hope to continue to build their lives.

The next day, my friend arrived in town. I wasn't expecting her to be there so early, but she was, and she was *ready* to go. I got myself together and went to meet her. Surprisingly, it was this moment in time, the conversation that was just ahead of me that would begin to wake me up and shift my thinking. We sat and ate kale and I listened to her. I like to listen to people. As she spoke, I reflected on the years that we had been together at WDS, and thought about our growth, our friendship, and how we'd both changed over the years.

When I first met her she was, to say the least, a *little* uptight. A straight-laced, typical New Englander. No sign of meditation, no sign of prayer, no sign of yoga, no sign of green tea, no sign of kale. She was *not* listening to her inner voice, or connected to her soul's calling, but then I saw everything change. She sat in front of me, telling me about her meditation practice while she ate kale, and sipped some green drink. *Grace Happens*. I couldn't believe it, but it was happening.

One of the things I love about my job and about being in relationships with other humans is that I can hear and see the changes in their lives. She had changed, and I was (and still am) so happy for her. I was inspired. She had learned how to tap in-tune in-and turn on, it was brilliant! She was reaching for more in her life, and discovering unknown places, pushing her body, mind, and spirit to her unexplored edges.

Going to WDS and being in Portland was an answer to a prayer I had sent up months before when I was crying in my bathroom, one more time from pain and anxiety. I wanted to be given new perspective so that I could finish the request of a guide book on helping women to their most powerful tool, their inner voice. I also needed my own inner voice to be pushed back to the surface.

A constant theme in life when we are not connected to our inner voice, the Soul's Calling, is that life is *going* to happen. I want you to repeat this next sentence, "Life happens to me if I don't make life happen for me." My dear friend's life was happening, as she wanted and created.

I mentioned earlier that I was building a house. Four years ago, I thought it was a good idea to buy a house and redo it here in San Francisco, California. Now, if nobody's ever told you, or you've never experienced rebuilding a home from the ground up, I want to share with you that it is a spiritual experience especially if you have a partner or spouse who is a perfectionist.

Before my husband and I purchased our one-day-dream-house, I felt we were reasonably connected, on the *same page*, and reaching for similar things and goals in life. Creating a house from the ground up is hard. It's no joke when they say building a home can tear a marriage apart. Year one of building the house was easy; year two simple; year three is when we found dangerous ground. When you don't agree on tile, and you're over budget by $XXX how do you make a sacrifice? How do you compromise? How do you give up when everything inside of you tells you to persevere?

Building our house destroyed me. It's made me look at my husband differently; it's made me look at myself differently and how I selfishly operate in daily living. We are in the house now, and a couple of weeks ago, I looked around and realized that together, we created art. We built something together, we co-created, and we have a masterpiece. Everyone tells us our house is stunning, but stunning doesn't matter when you're heart is broken.

It looks good on the inside and the outside, but our marriage suffered, we suffered, I suffered. I neglected that deep Connection, my Soul's Desire. I've had plenty of time to sit quietly and look around at my house—at the beauty—yet I felt alone, and disconnected.

I have been reminded over and over again to get quiet and get in touch with how I feel.

Feelings manifest greater outcomes, not the other way around, feelings bring life to reality.

My feelings of isolation and unease brought precisely more

of that into my life. It was lonely, and as I mentioned earlier, my health issues grew out of proportion. When I'd get out of bed, my hips ached as if I were a ninety-year-old woman, and going down our stairs was a major daily feat. I'd mention it to my husband, and he would only look at me with disdain, wordless, no love. Something changed in our relationship and words cannot describe it. I suffered silently, and my family relationships deteriorated. I don't share this with you for pity, but to reveal that even someone who has been on a path can fall. When my lens of service fell from focus, I shifted, and havoc settled on my life. I see this so often with women.

The Obstacle: Prayer is not enough.

Life is a series of focal points. We see them daily and they change from moment to moment. My career path as a health coach was not what I craved and the *feeling* that I had for it was that of *exhaustion*—who wants to work with a coach who is exhausted? My focal point had changed.

I needed *something* to crack me open—I prayed. From that prayer, I decided to create a one-day "Wellness" workshop with a fellow artist and life coach. I had these grandiose ideas that this would bring the recognition that I was looking for in life.

> *Definition: Recognition: acknowledgment of something's existence, validity.*

Recognition is about validation, it's not about joy and happiness. I was heading in the wrong direction again; my pain grew.

She came over to my house one day while planning our workshop, she was her vibrant, lively-young-spirited self, bouncing with joy, smiling ear to ear. She recognized my pain and said, "I think I have something that will help you and your pain. Try this hemp oil."

I wanted nothing to do with this, as I will always protect my recovery, and I wasn't going to lose it over pot. I hate marijuana. She continued by explaining that this had nothing to do with pot and that I wasn't going to get "high." I gave her my all-knowing smile and said, "Ok, leave it for me. I'll share it with my husband. If it works for him, I'll try it." She pumped a couple of doses into a small plastic container and left them with me. We continued our planning.

A few days later I woke up one more time with debilitating pain. I stood in my bathroom, and looked down at the small container of hemp, and prayed, "Is this it? What if this is a *Divine* gift? What if this is what my body needs?" I got quiet, tuned in and listened. There she was, my gentle-polite-old friend, finally bubbling to the surface, my inner voice, yelled, "Try It." Hesitantly, I stuck my finger into the small container, feeling the oil and then placed it on my body, directly on the pain. I stood in front of the mirror, looking into my eyes asking for help, I'd been here before, desperate. I tapped in, tuned in, and turned on to the pain. It dissipated—it was odd. *I felt free.* I dropped to my knees and started to cry. The pain had gone from a nagging nine to a four, and it was easing up as the seconds passed. Now, I'm not going to say this was all about the hemp oil or all about a passing moment of spiritual intervention. What I am willing to say is that I stepped into a moment of alignment. At that moment, life changed, and I woke up once again.

The Truth: Time Changes Everything.

I began this journey, this book by sharing some intimate details of my life and my recovery with you and how I *thought* I was different. I'm not different. I took that one action, remember? I found hope through putting down a glass and finding my way to a lifestyle that has endless possibilities with millions of other women and men. Living in long term recovery from alcohol and drugs is hard. People begin to think, *oh she's ok, she's got it all together, look at her, no drink in sight.* Little do people understand that it's not alcohol that is the problem, it's the thinking and when you haven't had a drink or a mind-altering drug in 22+ years, one's thinking can and will backlash!

The mental illness named alcoholism is more prevalent today than even ten years ago, it is rampant amongst women who are trying to rise in the ranks, raise families, be solopreneurs and throughout college campuses and dormitories. It's everywhere: playgrounds, sandpits, sippy cups, and wine clubs are universally excepted means to *taking the edge off* and being okay. Drinking is not going away anytime soon. It's difficult for me to imagine a life without my drinking history, the endless sprees, the near-death experiences, and recovery from such a deadly substance, alcohol. I don't blame anyone for my disease or where every drank brought me.

Watching my mental illness come out of hibernation upon the birth of my son, as all of my hormones went sideways, was the beginning of uncharted territory. It awakened this untamed beast which I thought was locked in a cage for life, sadly I was wrong.

My recovery has been both rocky and smooth sailing after I woke up once again; I swore that I would treat my life differently. My disease is insidious and charming as Hannibal Lecter. There is no taking a break from my spiritual quest unless I want to be locked up with Hannibal! Not only do I have to pray, but I *must* meditate, connect with others and most importantly connect with Grace, the power that flows within when I plug in and listen. Grace Happens.

Since that conversation at WDS, finding hemp oil and not being lazy with my *spiritual practice*, life has changed. I'll start with my marriage, and although it's not rainbows and butterflies, it's not dead. I still look at him differently, yet in my heart I honor him. He is a man on a spiritual path so different than mine and I've found acceptance of him, of us. When I reflect on marrying my husband, I knew he was who he was, and that wasn't going to change: an agnostic at heart and an atheist at will. He would never seek what I *must* in order to evolve.

As a spiritual seeker and teacher, I walk a path with a man who doesn't share a vision even close to mine. *This is spiritual work*. When I took vows with my husband, I took them with all seriousness, as most humans do, right? I see the institution of marriage as a tool to higher ground, deeper learning. I look around and see so many broken homes, and look at my own past, coming from a household of parents who both gave up and dissolved marriage after marriage—between them they've tried and failed several times. Marriage is holy ground in the sense that as spiritual beings, we have *work* to do with Souls we meet up with and say *yes* to.

I see it as a duty, my Soul's journey to work out our differences, our likes, our visions. My marriage is a work in progress, my Soul's desire and being connected allows me to continue on the path, with him. Yes, it's uncomfortable, some days I think it's unbearable. But as a human having this spiritual experience, I know he has much to teach me; he has become one of my greatest teachers. My Soul's Desire keeps me present and reveals more to me every day, assuring the necessity of staying with him. Grace Happens.

Unexpected results occurred all around me, from changing one thing; is there **one** thing in your life you can change, now?

I never planned on using hemp as a part of my wellness experience. This plant ally, has taken me on a spiritual journey that I wasn't expecting.

My relationship with my son changed in endless, positive ways. It is painful to write and admit that it had become dreadful being with my son; two years ago when I felt like I was dying, I was becoming the mother that my judgment frowned upon. Today, I actually *want* to be with him and have changed the way I parent. I look forward to every moment I have with him, even his prepubescent attitude that makes me crazy. I no longer want to raise my hand at him, and I'm capable of talking through challenging moments. He kisses me at night and I know when he sleeps he is at peace, his body restores each night without added stress from what had become a regular shouting match.

The Truth: Healing is possible.

As my body regained health, and I became thirsty (again) for spiritual nutrients, I was able to dive back into meditation. During my meditation time I slowly began to see, hear, and feel how Adrian, my son, is such an integral part of my path, and how Grace shared him with me. He was never supposed to happen; I was told I would never have a child. His mere presence in my life every day is a gift and I'm now able to see it. Grace Happens.

Finding your Soul's Desire, your calling, can be an uphill battle, some days are easy while others you are crawling on your knees begging for mercy. I had many days of begging, but it was different after being introduced to the hemp oil and making a decision, again, to create a deeper practice of meditation. Remember back in chapter one and two where I shared about getting honest and accepting? Coming to this again, was the furthest thought on my mind—I simply didn't know what I didn't know. I couldn't see that everything that I *thought* I was working toward was everything that was tiring me out and depleting my Soul.

Getting honest, and awkwardly going deeper into unknown yet familiar spiritual realms, opened my eyes one more time to my Soul's calling. **Meditation.**

Why meditate?

As a part of every coaching sessions I introduce clients to a very scientific approach to meditation, Mindfulness Based Stress Reduction aka MBSR. I became a practitioner of MBSR because the science on mindfulness made an impact on me and it was incredibly easy method to share with the *non woo-woo* clients. Add hemp to the mix and results doubled. I was on to something. I began going deeper with my own practice. Stress melted away, and sleep revealed itself on a nightly basis, and for someone with insomnia or hormonal issues, sleep is a God Send.

Meditation is a practice. It's not something you buy once and use a couple of times; it's a gift that you give yourself every day that keeps on giving when you care for it. I didn't understand this. Within months of telling myself that I would treat my recovery differently, something happened, my twenty plus year meditation practice became stale as a Saltine. My practice wasn't working as I wanted it too, but I kept on with it. I sought through mediation to improve my contact, now that I had heard my inner voice again I wanted to go deeper. I studied quantum meditation, color therapy meditation, chakra meditation, sound baths, Shamanic Journey meditation, crystal vibration meditation; I even went so far as trying AMSR, and getting certified as a Reiki Practitioner. My inner voice was chanting with delight with each new tool I gathered to help more women step into alignment.

Then Yoga Nidra fell into my lap which was the answer to my seeking. I'm honored to share this practice with women for many reasons. The science of Yoga Nidra clearly shows a change in a woman's brain state on an EGG, coming out of high beta and allowing the participant to fall into alpha, theta, and even delta states. (This is incredible and life-changing!). It has been found to reduce tension and anxiety, help with PTSD, sleep disorders, hormonal issues, and so much more but most importantly it's been the quickest way for me and so many other women to connect to the inner voice. I hope you will join me in a session!

EXERCISE: Get quiet.

You have journeyed quite far on a rocky path. Rock eight settles on your truth.

Now is the time. Don't let one more minute pass you by without being whom you are meant to be on this planet. Sit for two minutes with a cup of tea and allow your thoughts to slow down as you stare out a window. Listen to the sounds around you and notice if anything shifts within.

Practice:

This planet and we humans, are facing incredibly challenging times ahead. Since my (re)awakening last year, I've tapped into watching and listening more deeply. Tuned into spiritual wisdom, centuries of the past, and lost, forgotten, unknown societies. I've turned on and stepped into the Universal Mind. The human is in trouble. What do you think about that? Another significant statement, right? Let me ask you this, do you feel pulled to make shifts, change lives, and speak up about something that is important to you? What you see, what you think, what you hear needs to be understood, now. We need help. I'm here to challenge you to stand up, take charge, and make the difference on this planet we need.

Over the next two weeks place your journal at your bedside to catch your dreams, write everything down upon awakening, give yourself time, schedule it, this is important. **Don't rush it**. You will be granted an extraordinary amount of information during this time. Your dreams hold answers to more significant obstacles, pay attention. You will know when to use this information at a later time, promise. Our dreams hold keys to different doors we are trying to find, open and close for safety. Again write it all down, even if it doesn't make any sense, and keep it.

As a woman, I want you to grasp that we are a life *force* this planet needs more of, and without us coming together we will fall; this planet will not survive what lies ahead at the rate in which we are orbiting. What I'm sharing may sound all too woo-woo for some, and if it does, put the book down now and focus on the first eight chapters. As I close this chapter, I'm inviting you to take your life and your vision to the next level and join me and other women in a community without judgment or criticism. Since stepping into this greater awakening, I don't have a choice in staying small and merely being a teacher, or a coach. Living a fearless life and being tapped into Grace has pushed me from the nest to gather women in seeking the world's solution. Stand with me and be bold. Bring your magic, your Soul's Calling, to the surface—now.

Have you been able to identify with any of the women's stories I've shared with in these chapters? If there's anything that I want in life, it is for you to find your strengths, your Desire, your Connectedness to be in the world as you dream, just as so many of my clients.

I found my purpose in life long ago, but as a human, I forgot, we forget, we are always growing—changing and entering new phases in life. You are growing and evolving; you may not even know it. Nothing is permanent. If you are unhappy, unsettled, or discontented, I hope you feel called —right now—to take action in your life. I implore you to find your True North, your Soul's Desire. Let *Grace Happen*. I know it's an ongoing process in our lives, but let's take this journey together.

Step in and find your inner voice. Uncover all the rocks on the path. Learn to be vulnerable, then learn to be even more vulnerable, you can and it's worth it. Get honest and choose acceptance, while cultivating your inner strength(s) to make the necessary changes the planet needs, now.

As I close this chapter, I am called to share one more inquiry with you: *What are you waiting for;* you have so much to give; let's do this, together!

I'm here with you always.

XO

LANE

INVITATION TO MORE RESOURCES

Feeling like you want to go further and can't quite tap in—don't worry I'm here for you with this Master Intuition Course or The Daily Practice.

(https://lanekennedy.com/master-your-intuition)

Grab the Daily Practice Course with discount code: **MOREPLEASE**

(https://lanekennedy.com/a-daily-practice)

Get on my calendar.

(https://lanekennedy.com/contact-lane)

Find a Workshop or Yoga Nidra Series with Me!

Order My Preferred Hemp Oil https://upgraded.primemybody.com/

Made in the USA
Monee, IL
11 August 2021